T[illegible]
CR[illegible]
OF
JESUS

One Of The Most Powerful Keys Of The Kingdom Of Heaven

JOHNSON AKINFENWA

The Cross of Jesus

Published by
Voice of Prophecy Publications
10 North Close
Dagenham
Essex
RM10 9LJ

All Scriptures, unless otherwise stated, are taken from the *King James Version* of the Bible.
Scriptures marked NKJV are from the *New King James Version.*
Scriptures marked AMP are from the *Amplified Bible.*
Scriptures marked AMPC are from the *Amplified Classic Bible.*
Scriptures marked NIV are from the *New International Version.*
Scriptures marked NLT are from the *New Living Translation.*
Scriptures marked ESV are from the *English Standard Version.*

ISBN 978-1-9997114-1-2

Cover design by Icon Media
Printed in the United Kingdom

CONTENTS

FOREWORD

The cross of Christ is the central message of the Christian faith. Take out the cross and all that we are left with is dead religion, lifeless rituals, and empty promises. The cross stands as the centrepiece of God's redemption programme for man and the cornerstone of man's relationship with God. These truths are the core message of this book.

Prophet Johnson shares the encounter he had with Christ, which refocused him on this message and gave him a mandate to share with the body of Christ. He roots the message in scripture and historical accounts and urges the last days' church to embrace the power and symbolism of the cross once again.

Surely, the preaching of the gospel is incomplete without the centrality of the cross and the sacrifice of

Christ that made an end to all sacrifices. To this end, Prophet Johnson's new book should be a blessing to this generation of believers and beyond.

Tokunbo Emmanuel

CEO, Sophos Books Ltd.

INTRODUCTION

And the key of the house of David I will lay upon his shoulder; he shall open and no one shall shut, he shall shut and no one shall open.
Isaiah 22:22 AMPC

Then Pilate turned Jesus over to them to be crucified. So they took Jesus away.
Carrying the cross by himself, he went to the place called Place of the Skull (in Hebrew, Golgotha).
John 19:16-17 NLT

On the 29th of October 2021, about 5:25pm, I was in the Kitchen to prepare a cup of hot lemon tea as part of my daily intake. I had just finished my afternoon prayer and my throat was a bit dry. Suddenly, I felt the presence of God around me, and heard the Lord speak to me. These are the words I heard Him say:

My Servant, note this: My second appearance will not be hastened until the message of the cross is prioritised and amplified above every other message and doctrinal teaching among My Ecclesia globally. My first appearance was fundamentally to fulfil the message, the process, and the price that I will pay on the cross to redeem and reconcile humanity back to God the Father. Furthermore, the consequence of what I accomplished on the cross in my first appearance will be the precursor determining the operations and the establishment of a new kingdom on the earth in my second appearance. All these were severally written in the Old Testament both in the Law, Psalms, and the Prophets. As you write, I will give you the highlights about why the message of the mystery of the cross is crucial and its significance to both My first and second coming.

THE LEVERAGING POWER OF THE CROSS AND THE BLOOD

The Lord further said to me that God the Father, from eternity, had set apart the LEVERAGING POWER of the cross and blood of Jesus to permanently defeat Satan and secure the redemption of humanity. This fact is substantiated by the Scripture that states that the Lamb of God was slain from the foundation of the world.

> *All who dwell on the earth will worship him, whose names have not been written in the Book of Life of the Lamb slain from the foundation of the world.*
> **Revelation 13:8 NKJV**

The Lord also revealed to me that the allegorical demonstration of the LEVERAGING POWER of the blood and the cross that secured redemption and deliverance of humanity from the power of darkness was demonstrated in Exodus 12.

In this text, we read that God wanted to deliver the children of Israel from the 400-year enslavement and oppression of Pharaoh and the Egyptians. The Lord instructed Moses to tell every man over a household to set apart a lamb that will be slain for their redemption. They were to use it as the Passover lamb and sprinkle its blood on the wooden pole of their doors. This is the allegory of the cross of Jesus and His blood. The children of Israel obeyed the instruction of Moses, and consequently, 3.5 million Israelites were delivered in one night. This fact is exemplified in the text below:

> 1 *Now the Lord spoke to Moses and Aaron in the land of Egypt, saying,*

2 *"This month shall be your beginning of months; it shall be the first month of the year to you.*
3 *Speak to all the congregation of Israel, saying: 'On the tenth of this month every man shall take for himself a lamb, according to the house of his father, a lamb for a household.*
4 *And if the household is too small for the lamb, let him and his neighbor next to his house take it according to the number of the persons; according to each man's need you shall make your count for the lamb.*
5 *Your lamb shall be without blemish, a male of the first year. You may take it from the sheep or from the goats.*
6 *Now you shall keep it until the fourteenth day of the same month. Then the whole assembly of the congregation of Israel shall kill it at twilight.*
7 *And they shall take some of the blood and put it on the two doorposts and on the lintel of the houses where they eat it.*
8 *Then they shall eat the flesh on that night; roasted in fire, with unleavened bread and with bitter herbs they shall eat it.*
9 *Do not eat it raw, nor boiled at all with water, but roasted in fire – its head with its legs and its entrails.*

10 You shall let none of it remain until
morning, and what remains of it until
morning you shall burn with fire.
11 And thus you shall eat it: with a belt on
your waist, your sandals on your feet, and
your staff in your hand. So you shall eat it
in haste. It is the Lord's Passover.
12 'For I will pass through the land of Egypt
on that night, and will strike all the
firstborn in the land of Egypt, both man
and beast; and against all the gods of Egypt
I will execute judgment: I am the Lord.
13 Now the blood shall be a sign for you on
the houses where you are. And when I see
the blood, I will pass over you; and the
plague shall not be on you to destroy you
when I strike the land of Egypt...
29 And it came to pass at midnight that the
Lord struck all the firstborn in the land of
Egypt, from the firstborn of Pharaoh who
sat on his throne to the firstborn of the
captive who was in the dungeon, and all
the firstborn of livestock.
30 So Pharaoh rose in the night, he, all his
servants, and all the Egyptians; and there
was a great cry in Egypt, for there was not
a house where there was not one dead.
31 Then he called for Moses and Aaron by
night, and said, "Rise, go out from among

my people, both you and the children of
Israel. And go, serve the Lord as you have
said.
32 *Also take your flocks and your herds, as*
you have said, and be gone; and bless me
also."
33 *And the Egyptians urged the people, that*
they might send them out of the land in
haste. For they said, "We shall all be dead."
34 *So the people took their dough before it*
was leavened, having their kneading bowls
bound up in their clothes on their
shoulders.
35 *Now the children of Israel had done*
according to the word of Moses, and they
had asked from the Egyptians articles of
silver, articles of gold, and clothing.
36 *And the Lord had given the people favor*
in the sight of the Egyptians, so that they
granted them what they requested. Thus
they plundered the Egyptians.
37 *Then the children of Israel journeyed*
from Rameses to Succoth, about six
hundred thousand men on foot, besides
children.
38 *A mixed multitude went up with them*
also, and flocks and herds – a great deal of
livestock.
39 *And they baked unleavened cakes of the*

dough which they had brought out of Egypt; for it was not leavened, because they were driven out of Egypt and could not wait, nor had they prepared provisions for themselves.
40 *Now the sojourn of the children of Israel who lived in Egypt was four hundred and thirty years.*
41 *And it came to pass at the end of the four hundred and thirty years – on that very same day – it came to pass that all the armies of the Lord went out from the land of Egypt.*
42 *It is a night of solemn observance to the Lord for bringing them out of the land of Egypt. This is that night of the Lord, a solemn observance for all the children of Israel throughout their generations.* **Exodus 12:1-13,29-43 NKJV**

In this revelation, I came to realise with a conviction that the CROSS became the symbol of everything that Christians stood for. Most importantly, it was the cross that facilitated reconciliation between God and humanity sealed by the blood of Jesus as exemplified in the passage below.

11 *Wherefore remember, that ye being in time past Gentiles in the flesh, who are*

called Uncircumcision by that which is called the Circumcision in the flesh made by hands;

[12] *That at that time ye were without Christ, being aliens from the commonwealth of Israel, and strangers from the covenants of promise, having no hope, and without God in the world:*

[13] *But now in Christ Jesus ye who sometimes were far off are made nigh by the blood of Christ.*

[14] *For he is our peace, who hath made both one, and hath broken down the middle wall of partition between us;*

[15] *Having abolished in his flesh the enmity, even the law of commandments contained in ordinances; for to make in himself of twain one new man, so making peace;*

[16] *And that he might reconcile both unto God in one body by the cross, having slain the enmity thereby.*

Ephesians 2:11-16

During the encounter, the Lord dictated to me twenty-three significant reasons why the message of the cross is pivotal and should be given more attention on our pulpits. These revelational truths will be the focus of the next chapter.

1

TWENTY-THREE SIGNIFICANT REVELATORY REASONS WHY THE MESSAGE OF THE CROSS IS PIVOTAL FOR THIS MOMENT IN THE CHURCH OF JESUS GLOBALLY

After the encounter I had with the Lord, Jesus commissioned me to teach this important message of the cross to the Church. This is a NOW message, and the Lord specifically instructed to start a pioneering work around the message in the United Kingdom. Below are the twenty-three statements the Lord dictated to me about the significance of the Cross.

Statement #1

In My first appearance, I came to the earth physically as God-Man primarily to go through suffering, lay down my life and shed my blood to atone for the sins of humanity and for their redemption, as declared in the books of the Law, the Psalms, and the Prophets.

[11] For the life of the flesh is in the blood: and I have given it to you upon the altar to make an atonement for your souls: for it is the blood that maketh an atonement for the soul.

Leviticus 17:11

[1] My God, my God, why hast thou forsaken me? why art thou so far from helping me, and from the words of my roaring?
[2] O my God, I cry in the day time, but thou hearest not; and in the night season, and am not silent.
[3] But thou art holy, O thou that inhabitest the praises of Israel.
[4] Our fathers trusted in thee: they trusted, and thou didst deliver them.
[5] They cried unto thee, and were delivered: they trusted in thee, and were not confounded.
[6] But I am a worm, and no man; a reproach of men, and despised of the people.
[7] All they that see me laugh me to scorn: they shoot out the lip, they shake the head, saying,
[8] He trusted on the LORD that he would deliver him: let him deliver him, seeing he delighted in him.
[9] But thou art he that took me out of the

*womb: thou didst make me hope when I was
upon my mother's breasts.*
10 *I was cast upon thee from the womb: thou
art my God from my mother's belly.*
11 *Be not far from me; for trouble is near; for
there is none to help.*
12 *Many bulls have compassed me: strong
bulls of Bashan have beset me round.*
13 *They gaped upon me with their mouths,
as a ravening and a roaring lion.*
14 *I am poured out like water, and all my
bones are out of joint: my heart is like wax;
it is melted in the midst of my bowels.*
15 *My strength is dried up like a potsherd;
and my tongue cleaveth to my jaws; and
thou hast brought me into the dust of death.*
16 *For dogs have compassed me: the
assembly of the wicked have inclosed me:
they pierced my hands and my feet.*
17 *I may tell all my bones: they look and
stare upon me.*
18 *They part my garments among them,
and cast lots upon my vesture.*
19 *But be not thou far from me, O LORD: O
my strength, haste thee to help me.*
20 *Deliver my soul from the sword; my
darling from the power of the dog.*
21 *Save me from the lion's mouth: for thou
hast heard me from the horns of the
unicorns.*

22 I will declare thy name unto my brethren: in the midst of the congregation will I praise thee.
23 Ye that fear the LORD, praise him; all ye the seed of Jacob, glorify him; and fear him, all ye the seed of Israel.
24 For he hath not despised nor abhorred the affliction of the afflicted; neither hath he hid his face from him; but when he cried unto him, he heard.
25 My praise shall be of thee in the great congregation: I will pay my vows before them that fear him.
26 The meek shall eat and be satisfied: they shall praise the LORD that seek him: your heart shall live for ever.
27 All the ends of the world shall remember and turn unto the LORD: and all the kindreds of the nations shall worship before thee.
28 For the kingdom is the LORD's: and he is the governor among the nations.
29 All they that be fat upon earth shall eat and worship: all they that go down to the dust shall bow before him: and none can keep alive his own soul.
30 A seed shall serve him; it shall be accounted to the Lord for a generation.
31 They shall come, and shall declare his

*righteousness unto a people that shall be
born, that he hath done this.*

Psalm 22:1-31

1 *Who hath believed our report? and to
whom is the arm of the LORD revealed?*
2 *For he shall grow up before him as a
tender plant, and as a root out of a dry
ground: he hath no form nor comeliness;
and when we shall see him, there is no
beauty that we should desire him.*
3 *He is despised and rejected of men; a man
of sorrows, and acquainted with grief: and
we hid as it were our faces from him; he was
despised, and we esteemed him not.*
4 *Surely he hath borne our griefs, and
carried our sorrows: yet we did esteem him
stricken, smitten of God, and afflicted.*
5 *But he was wounded for our transgressions,
he was bruised for our iniquities: the
chastisement of our peace was upon him;
and with his stripes we are healed.*
6 *All we like sheep have gone astray; we
have turned every one to his own way; and
the LORD hath laid on him the iniquity of
us all.*
7 *He was oppressed, and he was afflicted,
yet he opened not his mouth: he is brought
as a lamb to the slaughter, and as a sheep*

before her shearers is dumb, so he openeth not his mouth.
8 *He was taken from prison and from judgment: and who shall declare his generation? for he was cut off out of the land of the living: for the transgression of my people was he stricken.*
9 *And he made his grave with the wicked, and with the rich in his death; because he had done no violence, neither was any deceit in his mouth.*
10 *Yet it pleased the LORD to bruise him; he hath put him to grief: when thou shalt make his soul an offering for sin, he shall see his seed, he shall prolong his days, and the pleasure of the LORD shall prosper in his hand.*
11 *He shall see of the travail of his soul, and shall be satisfied: by his knowledge shall my righteous servant justify many; for he shall bear their iniquities.*
12 *Therefore will I divide him a portion with the great, and he shall divide the spoil with the strong; because he hath poured out his soul unto death: and he was numbered with the transgressors; and he bare the sin of many, and made intercession for the transgressors.*

Isaiah 53:1-12

Statement #2

I was made a scape goat to pacify God's anger and to pay for the sins of Adam and humanity.

> [11] *For the life of a creature is in the blood, and I have given it to you to make atonement for yourselves on the altar; it is the blood that makes atonement for one's life.*
> **Leviticus 17:11 NIV**

> [21] *For God made Christ, who never sinned, to be the offering for our sin, so that we could be made right with God through Christ.*
> **2 Corinthians 5:21 NLT**

Prophet Zechariah was given the message that the fountain of the blood of Jesus will be opened on the cross for the cleansing and the atonement of sins.

> *In that day a fountain shall be opened for the house of David and for the inhabitants of Jerusalem, for sin and for uncleanness.*
> **Zechariah 13:1-2**

John the Baptist was given the message of the cross when he introduced Jesus to the people as the Lamb of God who takes away the sins of the world.

29 The next day John saw Jesus coming toward him and said, "Look, the Lamb of God, who takes away the sin of the world!
30 This is the one I meant when I said, 'A man who comes after me has surpassed me because he was before me.'
31 I myself did not know him, but the reason I came baptizing with water was that he might be revealed to Israel.
John 1:29-31

Statement #3

It was on the cross that I executed judgement and defeated Satan and all the principalities and powers, and I have handed over to my Church the victory won on the cross.

31 Now is the judgment of this world: now shall the prince of this world be cast out.
32 And I, if I be lifted up from the earth, will draw all men unto me.
33 This he said, signifying what death he should die.
John 12:31-33

50 Jesus, when he had cried again with a loud voice, yielded up the ghost.
51 And, behold, the veil of the temple was rent in twain from the top to the bottom;

and the earth did quake, and the rocks rent;
52 *And the graves were opened; and many bodies of the saints which slept arose,*
53 *And came out of the graves after his resurrection, and went into the holy city, and appeared unto many.*
Matthew 27:50-53

18 *And Jesus came and said to them, "All authority in heaven and on earth has been given to me.*
19 *Go therefore and make disciples of all nations, baptizing them in the name of the Father and of the Son and of the Holy Spirit,*
20 *teaching them to observe all that I have commanded you. And behold, I am with you always, to the end of the age."*
Matthew 28:18-20 ESV

Statement #4

I fought all my battles against the prince of this world (Satan) on the cross. I executed judgement against the unrighteous Babylonian systems of this world on the cross and fought to secure the liberty and destiny of humanity from the enslavement and oppression of the prince of this world. As result of the battle on the cross I triumphed gloriously, having atoned for the sin of

the whole world to effect reconciliation between God and man.

31 Now judgment is upon this world [the sentence is being passed]. Now the ruler of this world (Satan) will be cast out.
32 And I, if and when I am lifted up from the earth [on the cross], will draw all people to Myself [Gentiles, as well as Jews]."
33 He said this to indicate the kind of death by which He was to die.
John 12:31-33 AMP

13 And you, being dead in your sins and the uncircumcision of your flesh, hath he quickened together with him, having forgiven you all trespasses;
14 Blotting out the handwriting of ordinances that was against us, which was contrary to us, and took it out of the way, nailing it to his cross;
15 And having spoiled principalities and powers, he made a shew of them openly, triumphing over them in it.
16 Let no man therefore judge you in meat, or in drink, or in respect of an holyday, or of the new moon, or of the sabbath days:
Colossians 2:13-16

Statement #5

The angels and the hosts of Heaven welcomed Me to My rightful position at the right hand of My Father in heaven with the song based upon what I accomplished on the cross, where I shed My blood to redeem humanity.

8 *And when he had taken the book, the four beasts and four and twenty elders fell down before the Lamb, having every one of them harps, and golden vials full of odours, which are the prayers of saints.*
9 *And they sung a new song, saying, Thou art worthy to take the book, and to open the seals thereof: for thou wast slain, and hast redeemed us to God by thy blood out of every kindred, and tongue, and people, and nation;*
10 *And hast made us unto our God kings and priests: and we shall reign on the earth.*
11 *And I beheld, and I heard the voice of many angels round about the throne and the beasts and the elders: and the number of them was ten thousand times ten thousand, and thousands of thousands;*
12 *Saying with a loud voice, Worthy is the Lamb that was slain to receive power, and riches, and wisdom, and strength, and*

honour, and glory, and blessing.
Revelation 5:8-12

Statement #6

It was on the cross that I facilitated reconciliation between God and man when I shed My blood for the redemption of humanity.

11 *Wherefore remember, that ye being in time past Gentiles in the flesh, who are called Uncircumcision by that which is called the Circumcision in the flesh made by hands;*
12 *That at that time ye were without Christ, being aliens from the commonwealth of Israel, and strangers from the covenants of promise, having no hope, and without God in the world:*
13 *But now in Christ Jesus ye who sometimes were far off are made nigh by the blood of Christ.*
14 *For he is our peace, who hath made both one, and hath broken down the middle wall of partition between us;*
15 *Having abolished in his flesh the enmity, even the law of commandments contained in ordinances; for to make in himself of twain one new man, so making peace;*
16 *And that he might reconcile both unto*

God in one body by the cross, having slain the enmity thereby.

Ephesians 2:11-16

[19] *For it pleased the Father that in him should all fulness dwell;*
[20] *And, having made peace through the blood of his cross, by him to reconcile all things unto himself; by him, I say, whether they be things in earth, or things in heaven.*
[21] *And you, that were sometime alienated and enemies in your mind by wicked works, yet now hath he reconciled*
22 In the body of his flesh through death, to present you holy and unblameable and unreproveable in his sight.

Colossians 1:19-22

Statement #7

The fountain of eternal abundant life, truth and grace in my blood was opened on the cross to save humanity. It was on the same cross that the fountain of the cleansing power in my blood was opened for the cleansing of the sins of idolatry, sins of false prophecy, and unrighteousness of men, and destruction of the activities of unclean spirit in the nations around the world.

[15] *so he will sprinkle many nations...*
Isaiah 52:15 NIV

[1] *In that day there shall be a fountain opened to the house of David and to the inhabitants of Jerusalem for sin and for uncleanness.*
[2] *And it shall come to pass in that day, saith the LORD of hosts, that I will cut off the names of the idols out of the land, and they shall no more be remembered: and also I will cause the prophets and the unclean spirit to pass out of the land.*
Zechariah 13:1-2

[33] *But when they came to Jesus, and saw that he was dead already, they brake not his legs:*
[34] *But one of the soldiers with a spear pierced his side, and forthwith came there out blood and water.*
John 19:33-34

From the passage we notice that the fountain was opened when the soldier pierced through the side of Jesus. As the blood of Jesus dripped to the ground, the power of the grave was destroyed, the principalities of death and corruption were defeated. For this reason, the righteous men and women who had served God faithfully in the Old Testament rose up from the grave having been delivered from the grip of death... Hallelujah!

> 50 *Jesus, when he had cried again with a loud voice, yielded up the ghost.*
> 51 *And, behold, the veil of the temple was rent in twain from the top to the bottom; and the earth did quake, and the rocks rent;*
> 52 *And the graves were opened; and many bodies of the saints which slept arose,*
> 53 *And came out of the graves after his resurrection, and went into the holy city, and appeared unto many.*
> **Matthew 27:50-53**

Statement #8

The quickening power of resurrection inherently embedded in My blood was responsible for the resurrection of My dead Body from the power of death and My ascension to the heavenly places, where I am now seated at the right hand of My Father, carrying My blood-bought Church along through the spirit of grace.

> 4 *But God, who is rich in mercy, for his great love wherewith he loved us,*
> 5 *even when we were dead in sins, hath quickened us together with Christ, (by grace ye are saved;)*

[6] *and hath raised us up together, and made us sit together in heavenly places in Christ Jesus.*
Ephesians 2:4-7

[23] *this Man, when handed over [to the Roman authorities] according to the predetermined decision and foreknowledge of God, you nailed to a cross and put to death by the hands of lawless and godless men.*
[24] *But God raised Him up, releasing Him and bringing an end to the agony of death, since it was impossible for Him to be held in death's power.*
Acts 2:23-24 AMP

[20] *Now the God of peace, that brought again from the dead our Lord Jesus, that great shepherd of the sheep, through the blood of the everlasting covenant,*
[21] *Make you perfect in every good work to do his will, working in you that which is wellpleasing in his sight, through Jesus Christ; to whom be glory for ever and ever. Amen.*
Hebrews 13:20-21

[10] *For we are His workmanship [His own master work, a work of art], created in*

Christ Jesus [reborn from above spiritually transformed, renewed, ready to be used] for good works, which God prepared [for us] beforehand [taking paths which He set], so that we would walk in them [living the good life which He prearranged and made ready for us].

Ephesians 2:10 AMP

Statement #9

The message of the cross will guarantee the assurance and evidence of My second coming because people will see the scars of where I was pierced through the palm of my hands and side, where the blood gushed out of Me. The scars will remain the same when I appear in my second coming.

25 *So the other disciples told him, "We have seen the Lord!" But he said to them, "Unless I see the nail marks in his hands and put my finger where the nails were, and put my hand into his side, I will not believe."*

26 *A week later his disciples were in the house again, and Thomas was with them. Though the doors were locked, Jesus came and stood among them and said, "Peace be with you!"*

[27] *Then he said to Thomas, "Put your finger here; see my hands. Reach out your hand and put it into my side. Stop doubting and believe."*

John 20:25-27

[7] *Behold, he cometh with clouds; and every eye shall see him, and they also which pierced him: and all kindreds of the earth shall wail because of him. Even so, Amen.*
[8] *I am Alpha and Omega, the beginning and the ending, saith the Lord, which is, and which was, and which is to come, the Almighty.*

Revelation 1:7-8

Statement #10

It was on the cross that I made atonement for the sins of humanity in order to revoke the global curse of poverty and hard labour that My Father pronounced on Adam. It was also on the cross that I was made a sacrificial sin offering so that the blessings of Abraham and the righteousness of God can be imputed upon man.

[17] *To Adam he said, "Because you listened to your wife and ate fruit from the tree about which I commanded you, 'You must not eat from it,' "Cursed is the ground*

because of you; through painful toil you
will eat food from it all the days of your life.
18 It will produce thorns and thistles for
you, and you will eat the plants of the field.
19 By the sweat of your brow you will eat
your food until you return to the ground,
since from it you were taken; for dust you
are and to dust you will return."

Genesis 3:17-19 NIV

13 Christ hath redeemed us from the curse of
the law, being made a curse for us: for it is
written, Cursed is every one that hangeth
on a tree:
14 That the blessing of Abraham might come
on the Gentiles through Jesus Christ; that
we might receive the promise of the Spirit
through faith.

Galatians 3:13-14

21 For God made Christ, who never sinned,
to be the offering for our sin, so that we
could be made right with God through
Christ.

Corinthians 5:21 NLT

30 But it is from Him that you are in Christ
Jesus, who became to us wisdom from God
[revealing His plan of salvation], and
righteousness [making us acceptable to

God], and sanctification [making us holy and setting us apart for God], and redemption [providing our ransom from the penalty for sin].
1 Corinthians 1:30 AMP

Statement #11
It was on My way to the cross and when I was hung on the cross that the power of the principality of poverty was defeated and destroyed. I was stripped naked, and the crown of thorns was placed on My head so that My grace for abundant riches and financial prosperity may be released upon man.

27 Then the soldiers of the governor took Jesus into the common hall, and gathered unto him the whole band of soldiers.
28 And they stripped him, and put on him a scarlet robe.
29 And when they had platted a crown of thorns, they put it upon his head, and a reed in his right hand: and they bowed the knee before him, and mocked him, saying, Hail, King of the Jews!...
35 And they crucified him, and parted his garments, casting lots: that it might be fulfilled which was spoken by the prophet,

They parted my garments among them, and upon my vesture did they cast lots.
Matthew 27:27-29,35

[9] *You know the generous grace of our Lord Jesus Christ. Though he was rich, yet for your sakes he became poor, so that by his poverty he could make you rich.*
2 Corinthians 8:9 NLT

[8] *And God is able to make all grace abound toward you; that ye, always having all sufficiency in all things, may abound to every good work:*
[9] *(As it is written, He hath dispersed abroad; he hath given to the poor: his righteousness remaineth for ever.*
[10] *Now he that ministereth seed to the sower both minister bread for your food, and multiply your seed sown, and increase the fruits of your righteousness;)*
[11] *Being enriched in everything to all bountifulness, which causeth through us thanksgiving to God.*
2 Corinthians 9:8-11

Statement #12

The blood of My cross secured believers' access key to the presence of the Father in the Holy of Holies that they might offer acceptable and true worship.

23 *But a time is coming and is already here when the true worshipers will worship the Father in spirit [from the heart, the inner self] and in truth; for the Father seeks such people to be His worshipers.*
24 *God is spirit [the Source of life, yet invisible to mankind], and those who worship Him must worship in spirit and truth."*

John 4:23-24 AMP

19 *Therefore, believers, since we have confidence and full freedom to enter the Holy Place [the place where God dwells] by [means of] the blood of Jesus,*
20 *by this new and living way which He initiated and opened for us through the veil [as in the Holy of Holies], that is, through His flesh,*
21 *and since we have a great and wonderful Priest [Who rules] over the house of God,*
22 *let us approach [God] with a true and sincere heart in unqualified assurance of faith, having had our hearts sprinkled clean from an evil conscience and our bodies washed with pure water.*
23 *Let us seize and hold tightly the confession of our hope without wavering, for He who promised is reliable and*

trustworthy and faithful [to His word].
Hebrews 10:19-23 AMP

Statement #13
The major lyrics of all the worship songs in heaven before the throne of God the Father and My throne is about what happened on the cross where I sacrificed My blood for the redemption of man as the Lamb of God that was slain.

8 *And when He had taken the scroll, the four living creatures and the twenty-four elders fell down before the Lamb (Christ), each one holding a harp and golden bowls full of fragrant incense, which are the prayers of the saints (God's people).*
9 *And they sang a new song [of glorious redemption], saying,*
"Worthy and deserving are You to take the scroll and to break its seals; for You were slain (sacrificed), and with Your blood You purchased people for God from every tribe and language and people and nation.
10 *"You have made them to be a kingdom [of royal subjects] and priests to our God; and they will reign on the earth."*
Revelation 5:8-10 AMP

Statement #14
Through My victorious death on the cross and resurrection, I was able to recover what Satan stole from Adam and restored it back to Church as redemptive blessings.

3 Blessed and worthy of praise be the God and Father of our Lord Jesus Christ, who has blessed us with every spiritual blessings in the heavenly realms in Christ.
Ephesians 1:3 AMP

16 For by him were all things created, that are in heaven, and that are in earth, visible and invisible, whether they be thrones, or dominions, or principalities, or powers: all things were created by him, and for him:
17 And he is before all things, and by him all things consist.
18 And he is the head of the body, the church: who is the beginning, the firstborn from the dead; that in all things he might have the preeminence.
19 For it pleased the Father that in him should all fulness dwell;
20 And, having made peace through the blood of his cross, by him to reconcile all things unto himself; by him, I say, whether they be things in earth, or things in heaven.
21 And you, that were sometime alienated

and enemies in your mind by wicked works, yet now hath he reconciled
22 *In the body of his flesh through death, to present you holy and unblameable and unreproveable in his sight.*
Colossians 1:16-22

21 *For God made Christ, who never sinned, to be the offering for our sin, so that we could be made right with God through Christ.*
2 Corinthians 5:21 NLT

10 *"You have made them to be a kingdom [of royal subjects] and priests to our God; and they will reign on the earth."*
11 *Then I looked, and I heard the voice of many angels around the throne and [the voice] of the living creatures and the elders; and they numbered myriads of myriads, and thousands of thousands (innumerable),*
12 *saying in a loud voice, "Worthy and deserving is the Lamb that was sacrificed to receive power and riches and wisdom and might and honor and glory and blessing."*
Revelation 5:10-12 AMP

Statement #15

Prophet Zechariah was given the message of the cross that the fountain of My blood will be opened

on the cross for the cleansing and the atonement of sins of humanity and that this phenomenon will happen in Jerusalem. Likewise, John the Baptist was given the message of the cross when he introduced Me to the people as the Lamb of God who takes away the sins of the world.

> [1] *In that day a fountain shall be opened for the house of David and for the inhabitants of Jerusalem, for sin and for uncleanness.* **Zechariah 13:1**

> [29] *The next day John saw Jesus coming toward him and said, "Look, the Lamb of God, who takes away the sin of the world!*
> [30] *This is the one I meant when I said, 'A man who comes after me has surpassed me because he was before me.'*
> [31] *I myself did not know him, but the reason I came baptizing with water was that he might be revealed to Israel.*
> **John 1:29-31**

Statement #16

The Lord spoke to me that He (Jesus) personally preached and prophesied about the message of His own cross.

> [14] *Just as Moses lifted up the [bronze] serpent in the desert [on a pole], so must the Son of*

Man be lifted up [on the cross],
15 so that whoever believes will in Him have eternal life [after physical death, and will actually live forever].
John 3:14-15 AMP

31 Now judgment is upon this world [the sentence is being passed]. Now the ruler of this world (Satan) will be cast out.
32 And I, if and when I am lifted up from the earth [on the cross], will draw all people to Myself [Gentiles, as well as Jews]."
33 He said this to indicate the kind of death by which He was to die.
John 12:31-33AMP

Statement #17

The cross has become the tree of life which Adam and Eve were forbidden to partake of again. On the Cross I became the fruit of life while the cross became the tree of life.

22 And the LORD God said, "The man has now become like one of us, knowing good and evil. He must not be allowed to reach out his hand and take also from the tree of life and eat, and live forever."
23 So the LORD God banished him from the

Garden of Eden to work the ground from which he had been taken.
Genesis 3:22-23 NIV

[45] *From noon until three in the afternoon darkness came over all the land.*
[46] *About three in the afternoon Jesus cried out in a loud voice, "Eli, Eli, lema sabachthani?" (meaning "My God, my God, why have you forsaken me?").*
[47] *When some of those standing there heard this, they said, "He's calling Elijah."*
[48] *Immediately one of them ran and got a sponge. He filled it with wine vinegar, put it on a staff, and offered it to Jesus to drink.*
[49] *The rest said, "Now leave him alone. Let's see if Elijah comes to save him."*
[50] *And when Jesus had cried out again in a loud voice, he gave up his spirit.*
Matthew 27:45-53 NIV

Statement #18

It was My death on the cross that facilitated, secured, and guaranteed the conferment on Me by My Father all AUTHORITY AND POWER in heaven, on the earth, and beneath the earth.

[8] *And being found in appearance as a man, He humbled Himself and became obedient*

to the point of death, even the death of the cross.
[9] *Therefore God also has highly exalted Him and given Him the name which is above every name,*
[10] *that at the name of Jesus every knee should bow, of those in heaven, and of those on earth, and of those under the earth,*
[11] *and that every tongue should confess that Jesus Christ is Lord, to the glory of God the Father.*
Philippians 2:8-11 NKJV

[1] *Therefore we also, since we are surrounded by so great a cloud of witnesses, let us lay aside every weight, and the sin which so easily ensnares us, and let us run with endurance the race that is set before us,*
[2] *looking unto Jesus, the author and finisher of our faith, who for the joy that was set before Him endured the cross, despising the shame, and has sat down at the right hand of the throne of God.*
Hebrews 12:1-2 NKJV

Statement #19

There were certain ancient scrolls written and sealed from eternity that could not be opened until I was slain on the cross to shed My blood for the

redemption of mankind from all nations, tribe, language, and tongue.

> [9] *And they sang a new song, saying: "You are worthy to take the scroll, And to open its seals; For You were slain, And have redeemed us to God by Your blood Out of every tribe and tongue and people and nation,*
> [10] *And have made us kings and priests to our God; And we shall reign on the earth."*
> **Revelation 5:9-10 NKJV**

Statement #20

Wherever the message of the Cross is given less attention or is grossly de-emphasised, it gives room for the attack and the influence of My adversary (Satan) to be stronger, thus overwhelming and weakening the effectiveness of My Church in any generation.

This situation is evident when the message about materialism, idolising church leaders as gods (Papalism, Fatherism); when the message of My grace is being abused; when the holy zeal to see My kingdom established and advanced wanes; when the fear of man and the systems of the world overwhelm the heart of believers/church (Leadership and Laity); when the laws of the nations are esteemed above My commandments in the Bible.

Further indication of the message of the cross include not given adequate attention is when believers earmark and spend less time with Me in their time of worship, prayer and service in their gathering; when the inner working of the Cross and my Spirit is not given appropriate attention to mould and shape individual believers according to my purpose; when righteousness and holy fear are not esteemed in the heart and attitude of believers, when My Church is run and administered as industry and by the wisdom of man and not as a ministry and as Kingdom of God on the earth. The appearance of all these indicators are signs that the message of the cross is grossly undervalued and given less attention on the pulpit.

The present state of My church now is like the state of the children of Israel in Shiloh, wherein the hearts of the priest were corrupt, their hearts were far away from God, manipulating people in taking tithes and offerings; they were spiritually dead without revelation and open vision from God; the truth of the word of God was very rare and the lamp of God was ebbing away. Alas!

> 12 *Now the sons of Eli were corrupt; they did not know the LORD.*
> 13 *And the priests' custom with the people was that when any man offered a sacrifice, the priest's servant would come with a three-pronged fleshhook in his hand while*

the meat was boiling.
14 *Then he would thrust it into the pan, or kettle, or caldron, or pot; and the priest would take for himself all that the fleshhook brought up. So they did in Shiloh to all the Israelites who came there.*
15 *Also, before they burned the fat, the priest's servant would come and say to the man who sacrificed, "Give meat for roasting to the priest, for he will not take boiled meat from you, but raw."*
16 *And if the man said to him, "They should really burn the fat first; then you may take as much as your heart desires," he would then answer him, "No, but you must give it now; and if not, I will take it by force."*
17 *Therefore the sin of the young men was very great before the LORD, for men abhorred the offering of the LORD.*
1 Samuel 2:12-17 NKJV

1 *And the child Samuel ministered unto the LORD before Eli. And the word of the LORD was precious in those days; there was no open vision.*
2 *And it came to pass at that time, when Eli was laid down in his place, and his eyes began to wax dim, that he could not see;*
3 *And ere the lamp of God went out in the temple of the LORD, where the ark of God*

was, and Samuel was laid down to sleep;
4 *That the LORD called Samuel: and he answered, Here am I.*
5 *And he ran unto Eli, and said, Here am I; for thou calledst me. And he said, I called not; lie down again. And he went and lay down.*
6 *And the LORD called yet again, Samuel. And Samuel arose and went to Eli, and said, Here am I; for thou didst call me. And he answered, I called not, my son; lie down again.*
7 *Now Samuel did not yet know the LORD, neither was the word of the LORD yet revealed unto him.*
1 Samuel 3:1-7

Statement #21

The Calendar of the years on the planet earth is chronicled and calculated relative to the day I was crucified on the cross. It was the day My Father set the calendar of New Beginning for humanity after the fall of Adam. It was on that the day I became the Passover Lamb as foreshadowed in the book of Exodus. This is the mystery behind the AD (After the Death of Christ) calendar.

1 *The LORD said to Moses and Aaron in Egypt,*
2 *"This month is to be for you the first*

month, the first month of your year.
3 *Tell the whole community of Israel that*
on the tenth day of this month each man is
to take a lamb for his family, one for each
household.
4 *If any household is too small for a whole*
lamb, they must share one with their
nearest neighbor, having taken into
account the number of people there are.
You are to determine the amount of lamb
needed in accordance with what each
person will eat.
5 *The animals you choose must be year-old*
males without defect, and you may take
them from the sheep or the goats.
6 *Take care of them until the fourteenth day*
of the month, when all the members of the
community of Israel must slaughter them
at twilight.
7 *Then they are to take some of the blood and*
put it on the sides and tops of the
doorframes of the houses where they eat the
lambs.
8 *That same night they are to eat the meat*
roasted over the fire, along with bitter
herbs, and bread made without yeast.
9 *Do not eat the meat raw or boiled in*
water, but roast it over a fire – with the
head, legs and internal organs.
10 *Do not leave any of it till morning; if*

some is left till morning, you must burn it.
11 *This is how you are to eat it: with your cloak tucked into your belt, your sandals on your feet and your staff in your hand. Eat it in haste; it is the LORD's Passover.*
Exodus 12:1-11 NIV

Jesus Christ, the Passover Lamb on the Cross, set a New Calendar for a New Beginning of New Relationship between God and man through Reconciliation by the blood of His cross.

45 *From noon until three in the afternoon darkness came over all the land.*
46 *About three in the afternoon Jesus cried out in a loud voice, "Eli, Eli, lema sabachthani?" (which means "My God, my God, why have you forsaken me?").*
47 *When some of those standing there heard this, they said, "He's calling Elijah."*
48 *Immediately one of them ran and got a sponge. He filled it with wine vinegar, put it on a staff, and offered it to Jesus to drink.*
49 *The rest said, "Now leave him alone. Let's see if Elijah comes to save him."*
50 *And when Jesus had cried out again in a loud voice, he gave up his spirit.*
Matthew 27:45-50 NIV

Statement #22
The Seal to open the Scroll for the establishment of the Church (Ecclesia) on the earth was broken on the day I was slain on the Cross. On this day, the pattern of the Ecclesia to be established on the earth was revealed to be comprised of the kings and priests that would govern the earth on behalf of God.

6 Then I saw a Lamb that looked as if it had been slaughtered, but it was now standing between the throne and the four living beings and among the twenty-four elders. He had seven horns and seven eyes, which represent the sevenfold Spirit of God that is sent out into every part of the earth.
7 He stepped forward and took the scroll from the right hand of the one sitting on the throne.
8 And when he took the scroll, the four living beings and the twenty-four elders fell down before the Lamb. Each one had a harp, and they held gold bowls filled with incense, which are the prayers of God's people.
9 And they sang a new song with these words: "You are worthy to take the scroll and break its seals and open it. For you were slaughtered, and your blood has ransomed people for God from every tribe

and language and people and nation.
[10] *And you have caused them to become a Kingdom of priests for our God. And they will reign on the earth."* **Revelation 5:6-10 NLT**

Statement #23

The day that the redemption price was paid on the cross, Satan was totally defeated and the certificate of death and debt by which Satan accused humanity because of the sins inherited from Adam was written off and nailed to the cross.

[15] *But there is a great difference between) Adam's sin and God's gracious gift. For the sin of this one man, Adam, brought death to many. But even greater is God's wonderful grace and his gift of forgiveness to many through this other man, Jesus Christ.*
Romans 5:15 NLT

[13] *When you were dead in your sins and in the uncircumcision of your flesh (worldliness, manner of life), God made you alive together with Christ, having [freely] forgiven us all our sins,*
[14] *having canceled out the certificate of debt consisting of legal demands [which were in force] against us and which were hostile*

to us. And this certificate He has set aside and completely removed by nailing it to the cross.
15 *When He had disarmed the rulers and authorities [those supernatural forces of evil operating against us], He made a public example of them [exhibiting them as captives in His triumphal procession], having triumphed over them through the cross.*
Colossians 2:13-15 AMP

Statement #24
The acts of Abraham and Isaac foreshadowed my day as I carried my cross upon my shoulder to Calvary, just as Isaac carried the slaughter wood on his shoulder to Mount Moriah.

6 *And Abraham took the wood of the burnt offering, and laid it upon Isaac his son; and he took the fire in his hand, and a knife; and they went both of them together.*
7 *And Isaac spake unto Abraham his father, and said, My father: and he said, Here am I, my son. And he said, Behold the fire and the wood: but where is the lamb for a burnt offering?*
8 *And Abraham said, My son, God will provide himself a lamb for a burnt offering: so they went both of them together.*

[9] *And they came to the place which God had told him of; and Abraham built an altar there, and laid the wood in order, and bound Isaac his son, and laid him on the altar upon the wood.*

Genesis 22:6-9

PRAYER:

I pray that God Almighty, through the Holy Spirit, will perfect the crushing effects of the power of the Cross in us to give us the same experience like the Apostle Paul:

[20] ***I have been crucified with Christ; it is no longer I who live, but Christ lives in me; and the life which I now live in the flesh I live by faith in the Son of God, who loved me and gave Himself for me.***

Galatians 2:20 NKJV

2

THE ARRAGEMENT OF THE ISRAELITES TRIBAL CAMPS AS AN ELLEGORY OF THE CALVARY CROSS

The more I desire to know about the message of the cross, the more the Holy Spirit takes me deeper into the revelation about the mystery and power of the cross. As I studied the word, the Holy Spirit brought my attention to the arrangement and the pattern of the camp of the children of Israel during their 40-year sojourn in the wilderness. It was astonishing what I discovered in the book of Numbers, particularly chapters two and three.

The LORD gave detailed instructions to Moses on how to arrange the children of Israel around the tabernacle as they journeyed to the promise land. I made a stunning discovery about the mystery behind the arrangement of the tribes, especially how each tribe will raise their standards/ensigns. In this arrangement, God revealed the allegory of the picture and shape of the Cross of Calvary. Hallelujah! A very careful observation will show that the pattern of the arrangement of the tribal camps allegorically reveals the shape of the CROSS. The cross of Calvary is also foreshadowed in the Old Testament as the Brazen Altar, according to the Exodus 27:1-2.

This revelation gives us insight into how God deal with His people, especially the Church. God will always give specific instructions about how He wants us to do certain things so we can get the right result. All His instructions are for our good if we intentionally align ourselves with them. I learnt from the study of Numbers chapters 2 and 3 that as the children of Israel followed the God-given arrangement of the pattern of their tribal camps, the glory of God was always among them as a pillar of fire by night and a pillar of cloud by day, irrespective of whether they were moving or camping.

There was a condition attached to the arrangement of the camp, which was the TRIBE OF JUDAH must lead from the EAST. We are going to see this pattern in the pictures below.

In other words, as the tribes of Israel maintained the pattern of THE CROSS in their camping, with the Tabernacle at the centre of the camp and the Ark positioned at its rightful place, administered accordingly by the Levites, the GLORY OF GOD automatically descended upon the camp, building a wall of fire around them in the night and a cloud during the day.

I believe with all my heart that if the church of Jesus Christ identifies fully with the message of the cross and walks in the reality of what Jesus accomplished on the CROSS, we can also experience the same glory wall of FIRE in the night and glory cloud during the day. Hallelujah!

> 1 *The LORD said to Moses and Aaron:*
>
> 2 *"The Israelites are to camp around the tent of meeting some distance from it, each of them under their standard and holding the banners of their family."*
>
> 3 *On the east, toward the sunrise, the divisions of the camp of Judah are to encamp under their standard. The leader of the people of Judah is Nahshon son of Amminadab.*
>
> 4 *His division numbers 74,600.*
>
> 5 *The tribe of Issachar will camp next to them. The leader of the people of Issachar is Nethanel son of Zuar.*
>
> 6 *His division numbers 54,400.*
>
> 7 *The tribe of Zebulun will be next. The leader of the people of Zebulun is Eliab son of Helon.*

[8] His division numbers 57,400.

[9] All the men assigned to the camp of Judah, according to their divisions, number 186,400. They will set out first.

[10] On the south will be the divisions of the camp of Reuben under their standard. The leader of the people of Reuben is Elizur son of Shedeur.

[11] His division numbers 46,500.

[12] The tribe of Simeon will camp next to them. The leader of the people of Simeon is Shelumiel son of Zurishaddai.

[13] His division numbers 59,300.

[14] The tribe of Gad will be next. The leader of the people of Gad is Eliasaph son of Deuel.

[15] His division numbers 45,650.

[16] All the men assigned to the camp of Reuben, according to their divisions, number 151,450. They will set out second.

[17] Then the tent of meeting and the camp of the Levites will set out in the middle of the camps. They will set out in the same order as they encamp, each in their own place under their standard.

[18] On the west will be the divisions of the camp of Ephraim under their standard. The leader of the people of Ephraim is Elishama

son of Ammihud.

19 *His division numbers 40,500.*

20 *The tribe of Manasseh will be next to them. The leader of the people of Manasseh is Gamaliel son of Pedahzur.*

21 *His division numbers 32,200.*

22 *The tribe of Benjamin will be next. The leader of the people of Benjamin is Abidan son of Gideoni.*

23 *His division numbers 35,400.*

24 *All the men assigned to the camp of Ephraim, according to their divisions, number 108,100. They will set out third.*

25 *On the north will be the divisions of the camp of Dan under their standard. The leader of the people of Dan is Ahiezer son of Ammishaddai.*

26 *His division numbers 62,700.*

27 *The tribe of Asher will camp next to them. The leader of the people of Asher is Pagiel son of Okran.*

28 *His division numbers 41,500.*

29 *The tribe of Naphtali will be next. The leader of the people of Naphtali is Ahira son of Enan.*

30 *His division numbers 53,400.*

31 *All the men assigned to the camp of Dan number 157,600. They will set out last, under their standards.*

32 *These are the Israelites, counted according to their families. All the men in the camps, by their divisions, number 603,550.*

33 *The Levites, however, were not counted along with the other Israelites, as the LORD commanded Moses.*

34 *So the Israelites did everything the LORD commanded Moses; that is the way they encamped under their standards, and that is the way they set out, each of them with their clan and family.*

Numbers 2:1-34 NIV

In my research, I discovered (on the website of Reason For Hope*Jesus who owns the Copyright) that the aerial view of the pattern of Israel's tribal camp arrangement, as described in the passage above, revealed or foreshadowed the prophetic sign of the "Calvary Cross." This mystery revealed the prophetic allegory of the 'cross' of calvary in an epoch proportion (see image below).

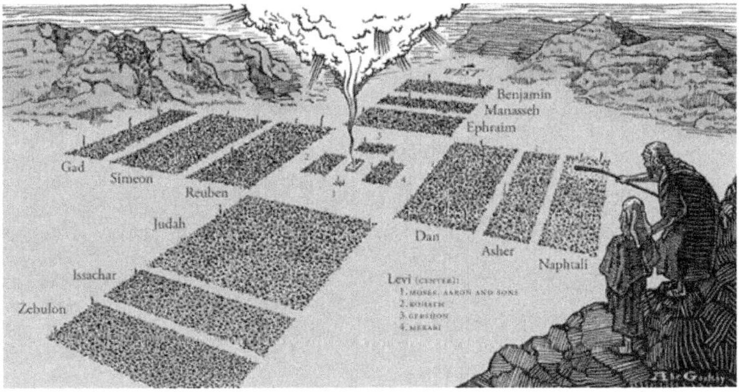

(Copyright: Reasons For Hope*Jesus)

If we consider the literal arrangement of the tribal camps, as ordered by God, when viewed from above, the encampment seems to form a cross. God's prescription of the tribal pattern allegorically foreshadowed the prophetic picture of the cross as the Brazen Altar of sacrifice for human redemption.

According to the passage in Numbers 2, the individual totals can be depicted as shown, yet the totals along the two axes (see below) do not agree with this picture. The East/West axis (representing the upright) totals 294,500 and the North/South axis (representing the horizontal beam) totals 309,050. The horizontal representation should be longer than the vertical. In addition, if the encampment arrangement is patterned after the order when the people move, the tribe of Judah is misplaced: Judah leads out and should be furthest from the centre, not the closest.

PICTURE TWO

The re-arrangement of the above picture showing East/West Axis to represent the upright and the North/South Axis representing the horizontal beam, will put the tribe of Judah at the rightful position thereby leading from the top of the East Axis (upright/ vertical beam) according to the description and interpretation of the content of Numbers chapters two. A more practical way of looking at the arrangement according to the passage would be to take the instructions to mean in the East, in the South, in the West, and in the North.

Therefore, when everyone moved, Judah could lead (Numbers 2:9) and the other tribes could follow in a single column, the most likely way of moving.

When a tribe's mother and birth order is factored, there is a distinct pattern:

East		
Tribe	Mother	Census
Judah	Leah 4	74,600
Issachar	Leah 5	54,400
Zebulun	Leah 6	57,400
		186,400

North		
Tribe	Mother	Census
Dan	Bilhah (R) 1	62,700
Asher	Zilpah (L) 2	41,500
Naphtali	Bilah (R) 2	53,400
		157,600

Levi - Leah 3 - 22,300

South		
Tribe	Mother	Census
Rueben	Leah 1	46,500
Simeon	Leah 2	59,300
Gad	Zilpah (L) 1	45,650
		151,450

West		
Tribe	Mother	Census
Ephraim	Rachel 1*	40,500
Manasseh	Rachel 1*	32,200
Benjamin	Rachel 2	35,400
		108,100

The North and South groups are made from only first and second born except Rachel's; the West group is made from Rachel's first and second sons; the East group from Leah's fourth, fifth, and sixth sons. Thus, there are three groups of first and second born sons, and one group of fourth, fifth, and sixth sons which "face" Levi, the only third son.

The above pattern therefore revealed the accurate and God's desired pattern, showing that Judah must always lead toward the East. This desired order was facilitated by the arrangement, using the factors of the mothers of the twelve tribes.

There is a powerful revelation here, which confirm the curse that God pronounced upon Satan in the Garden of Eden, when God said the seed of woman shall crush the head of Satan (permanent defeat on the cross). It was the women's factor that God used to design the order of the tribal camp of the children of Israel (which foreshadowed the CROSS OF JESUS where Satan and all his demons were eternally and permanently defeated).

> 15 *"And I will put enmity (open hostility) Between you and the woman, And between your seed (offspring) and her Seed; He shall [fatally] bruise your head, And you shall [only] bruise His heel."* **Genesis 3:15 AMP**

Even though Jesus sustained temporary "bruises" on the cross which healed on the third day of resurrection, Satan's head was crushed and permanently defeated by the seed of a woman. Hallelujah!

The death and resurrection of Jesus removed all the curses God pronounced on Adam and Eve.

> [13] *Christ purchased our freedom and redeemed us from the curse of the Law and its condemnation by becoming a curse for us—for it is written, "CURSED IS EVERYONE WHO HANGS [crucified] ON A TREE (cross)."*
>
> **Galatians 3:13 AMP**

Conversely, the crucifixion of Jesus on the cross and His resurrection inflicted major defeat on Satan and all his power in a triumphant procession.

> [13] *When you were dead in your sins and in the uncircumcision of your flesh (worldliness, manner of life), God made you alive together with Christ, having [freely] forgiven us all our sins,*
>
> [14] *having canceled out the certificate of debt consisting of legal demands [which were in*

force] against us and which were hostile to us. And this certificate He has set aside and completely removed by nailing it to the cross.

[15] *When He had disarmed the rulers and authorities [those supernatural forces of evil operating against us], He made a public example of them [exhibiting them as captives in His triumphal procession], having triumphed over them through the cross.*

Colossians 2:13-15 AMP

According to the camp arrangement and marching order, Judah must always lead towards the East direction. Anything contrary to this camp pattern will affect the move and the appearance of the presence and the glory of God. The Levites must be at the centre carrying all the furniture of the Tabernacle. In the same way wherever and whenever they stop for camping, the Levites and the priests will remain in the Tabernacle to administer sacrificial offerings day and night, thereby sustaining the Glory and the presence of God in the Camp.

The roles of the Levites were clearly stated in Numbers 3. They were exclusively to minster in and oversee the Tabernacle, which is at the centre of the camp. They were to take care of the sacrifices, offerings, Menorah, Shewbread, Altar of Incense, the Ark of Covenant etc.

With all these in mind, the Holy Spirit whispered to me clearly that the intensity of the coming manifestation of the glory of God among the Ecclesia will be directly proportional to their deeper understanding of the mystery of the finished work of Calvary. Presently, it seems the Church is only experiencing a partial eclipse of God's Glory due to a shallow understanding of the mystery of the cross.

The children of Israel marched to the promised land by the revelation of the power of the cross in their midst. They entered and got their inheritance in the promise land by the revelation of the power of the cross. They enjoyed the presence and the glory of God for forty years because they journeyed by the power of the cross. They were led and directed by the direction of the cross for forty years. They were surrounded and protected by the pillar of fire in the night and the cloud of glory in the day.

> 21 *The LORD went ahead of them. He guided them during the day with a pillar of cloud, and he provided light at night with a pillar of fire. This allowed them to travel by day or by night.*
>
> **Exodus 13:21 NLT**

> [105] *Your word is a lamp to guide my feet and a light for my path.*
>
> **Psalm 119:105 NLT**

When we walk with the Lord
In the light of His Word,
What a glory He sheds on our way;
While we do His good will,
He abides with us still,
And with all who will trust and obey.
Trust and obey, For there's no other way
To be happy in Jesus, But to trust and obey

Israel was led and directed by the direction of the cross for forty years until they got to the promise land. Their security and protection against their enemies was guaranteed day and night because the presence of Jehovah Gibor was in their midst.

Even when Ballack engaged Prophet Balaam to curse them, Balaam found it impossible to do so because of the power of the cross in the camp. Indeed, wherever the power of the cross is, there you will hear the voice of the Lion King of the tribe of Judah.

> [21] *No misfortune is seen in Jacob, no misery observed in Israel. The LORD their God is*

> *with them; the shout of the King is among them.*
>
> **Numbers 23:21NIV**

> 12 *Then the LORD spoke to you out of the fire. You heard the sound of words but saw no form; there was only a voice.*
>
> **Deuteronomy 4:12 NIV**

Israel's journey was by the direction of the tribe of the Lion of Judah according to God's instruction (Numbers 2:9). Halleluiah! Jesus, the Lion of the tribe of Judah, is the leader and the Commander-In-Chief of the Lord's armies, His church.

In fact, the Bible says that for our prayer to be answered, it must be prayed and aimed in the direction of the cross.

> 10 *And I will pour upon the house of David, and upon the inhabitants of Jerusalem, the spirit of grace and of supplications: and they shall look upon me whom they have pierced.*
>
> **Zechariah 12:10**

I believe the time is now when believers should be audaciously walking in the reality of our redemptive authority as kings, priests, and governors of the earth. And as we, the Ecclesia, begin to walk in this capacity based on our faith in the finished work of Calvary, the glory and the presence of God will always descend around us as pillar of Fire and cloud of Glory.

We are untouchable to the power of darkness. Why? The Bible says that we live move and have our being in Christ.

> [28] *For in him we live, and move, and have our being; as certain also of your own poets have said, For we are also his offspring.* **Acts 17:28**

In fact, the LORD promised to do it again for the children of Israel at Christ's second appearance, when the Commander-In-Chief of the Armies of Heaven will lead a battle that will wipe off all the enemies of the Jewish people once and for all, standing in their midst as the wall of fire.

> [5] *Then I, myself, will be a protective wall of fire around Jerusalem, says the LORD. And I will be the glory inside the city!* **Zechariah 2:5 NLT**

It was on the basis of God being the pillar of fire and cloud of glory around the children of Israel day and night that made Moses to write Psalm 91. All the promises in this Psalm are available for the church of Jesus today.

> 1 *He that dwelleth in the secret place of the most High shall abide under the shadow of the Almighty.*
>
> 2 *I will say of the LORD, He is my refuge and my fortress: my God; in him will I trust.*
>
> 3 *Surely he shall deliver thee from the snare of the fowler, and from the noisome pestilence.*
>
> 4 *He shall cover thee with his feathers, and under his wings shalt thou trust: his truth shall be thy shield and buckler.*
>
> 5 *Thou shalt not be afraid for the terror by night; nor for the arrow that flieth by day;*
>
> 6 *Nor for the pestilence that walketh in darkness; nor for the destruction that wasteth at noonday.*
>
> 7 *A thousand shall fall at thy side, and ten thousand at thy right hand; but it shall not come nigh thee.*
>
> 8 *Only with thine eyes shalt thou behold and see the reward of the wicked.*
>
> 9 *Because thou hast made the LORD, which*

is my refuge, even the most High, thy habitation;

10 *There shall no evil befall thee, neither shall any plague come nigh thy dwelling.*

11 *For he shall give his angels charge over thee, to keep thee in all thy ways.*

12 *They shall bear thee up in their hands, lest thou dash thy foot against a stone.*

13 *Thou shalt tread upon the lion and adder: the young lion and the dragon shalt thou trample under feet.*

14 *Because he hath set his love upon me, therefore will I deliver him: I will set him on high, because he hath known my name.*

15 *He shall call upon me, and I will answer him: I will be with him in trouble; I will deliver him, and honour him.*

16 *With long life will I satisfy him, and shew him my salvation.*

Psalm 91:1-16

3

THE SIGNIFICANCE OF THE BRAZEN ALTAR OF SACRIFICE AS THE SHADOW OF CALVARY CROSS

The journey to accessing God's presence and His glory starts from the Brazen Altar upon which blood sacrifices were carried out to atone for every sinful soul. This principle is upheld even till eternity. This Brazen Altar foreshadowed the cross of Calvary.

The Brazen Altar is so significant because it was the first article to be erected in the construction of the Tabernacle. Also significant is the fact that of all the articles of the Tabernacle, the consecration of the Brazen altar was the longest: it took twelve days (Numbers 7). Each of the twelve tribes of the children of Israel were drawn to and identified with the sacrifice on the Brazen altar (each tribe brought their sacrifice to the Brazen altar on different days). I believe this ritual was a sign of communion with

God and everlasting commitment of God to keep His eternal covenant with Israel.

This principal fact points to the statement by Jesus Christ in John 12:32 that once He is lifted up and slain on the cross, He will draw all men to Himself.

> [32] *And I, if I be lifted up from the earth, will draw all men unto me.*
>
> **John 12:32**

Special attention is given to the 'Brazen Altar' of sacrifice in the construction of the Tabernacle of Moses as described in Exodus 27:1-8:

> [1] *And thou shalt make an altar of shittim wood, five cubits long, and five cubits broad; the altar shall be foursquare: and the height thereof shall be three cubits.*
>
> [2] *And thou shalt make the horns of it upon the four corners thereof: his horns shall be of the same: and thou shalt overlay it with brass.*
>
> [3] *And thou shalt make his pans to receive his ashes, and his shovels, and his basons, and his fleshhooks, and his firepans: all the vessels thereof thou shalt make of brass.*

[4] And thou shalt make for it a grate of network of brass; and upon the net shalt thou make four brasen rings in the four corners thereof.

[5] And thou shalt put it under the compass of the altar beneath, that the net may be even to the midst of the altar.

[6] And thou shalt make staves for the altar, staves of shittim wood, and overlay them with brass.

[7] And the staves shall be put into the rings, and the staves shall be upon the two sides of the altar, to bear it.

[8] Hollow with boards shalt thou make it: as it was shewed thee in the mount, so shall they make it.

Exodus 27:1-8

In fact, I consider the Brazen altar to be the most important article of the Tabernacle. The reason for its significance is because the journey to God's presence starts from the Brazen Altar, which foreshadowed the Cross. In essence, the pathway to God's presence (Holy of Holies) is the Brazen Altar, which was a shadow of the cross of Calvary.

The first thing a man will see as he enters the gate of the Outer Court is the Brazen Altar. The sinful man would see this Altar, and before proceeding any further, he must identify with it. This Altar is a place of repentance and identification. It is the place where God, coming from heaven by the way of the Ark, meets with sinful man with an extended hand of forgiveness and grace. This Brazen Altar (in Hebrews "Mizbeach") means 'slaughter-place'. The sacrifice made upon this Altar symbolically typified the death of Jesus Christ.

NOTE: The fundamental truth here is that the entire worship of the children of Israel is determined by the quality of the prescribed sacrifice on the Brazen Altar. The blood shed on the altar is applied to the Mercy Seat, to the Horns of the altar of Incense, to every part of the Tabernacle, all the furniture, (Table of shewbread, Menorah…) and to the priests. Anyone associated with the solemn worship could only be part of it after the blood was applied.

Also amazing is the fact that the Tabernacle was built and erected at the centre of the "CROSS PATTERN" of the tribal camp arrangement.

No wonder Smith Wigglesworth wrote in one of his books that "there is no part of my body that is not covered by the blood of Jesus."

> [22] *And almost all things are by the law purged with blood; and without shedding of blood is no remission.*

[23] *It was therefore necessary that the patterns of things in the heavens should be purified with these; but the heavenly things themselves with better sacrifices than these.*

Hebrews 9:22-23

4

UNMASKING THE FOOLISHNESS, THE MYSTERY AND THE SIGNIFICANCE OF THE BRAZEN ALTAR (CALVARY CROSS)

[18] *For the preaching of the cross is to them that perish foolishness; but unto us which are saved it is the power of God.*
1 Corinthians 1:18

[16] *For I am not ashamed of the gospel of Christ: for it is the power of God unto salvation to everyone that believeth; to the Jew first, and also to the Greek.*
[17] *For therein is the righteousness of God revealed from faith to faith: as it is written, The just shall live by faith.*
Romans 1:16-17

The inspiration to write about this important topic has been building up in my spirit for many years. But recently, the Holy Spirit stirred me to put it down in writing because the revelation is meant for now. This mystery has been eternally concealed by God throughout the Old Testament to confound Satan and all his cohorts, the revelation of which is for the glory of the New Testament Triumphant Church.

Through the revelation of the Holy Spirit, we are privileged to download the mystery of the power of the cross and it relevant to our generation in the 21st century. This made us to become the custodians or the stewards of the mystery of the revealed words of God.

> [4] *So then, let us [who minister] be regarded as servants of Christ and stewards (trustees, administrators) of the mysteries of God [that He chooses to reveal].*
> **1 Corinthians 4:1 AMP**

> [2] *It is the glory of God to conceal a thing: but the honour of kings is to search out a matter.*
> **Proverbs 25:2**

> [8] *But there is a spirit in man: and the inspiration of the Almighty giveth them understanding.*
> **Job 32:8**

29 The secret things belong unto the LORD our God: but those things which are revealed belong unto us and to our children for ever, that we may do all the words of this law.

Deuteronomy 29:29

The mystery of the Calvary Cross was concealed in the Old Testament as the 'THE BRAZEN ALTAR OF SACRIFICE,' which I believe foreshadowed the CROSS OF CALVARY upon which Jesus will be crucified as the sacrificial Lamb of God who took away the sin of the whole world.

29 *The next day he saw Jesus coming to him and said, "Look! The Lamb of God who takes away the sin of the world!...*

36 *and he looked at Jesus as He walked along, and said, "Look! The Lamb of God!".*

John 1:29,36 AMP

The reason for the concealment of the mystery of the cross was revealed to the Apostle Paul as explained to the Corinthian Brethren. He let them know that the concealment of the mystery of the Cross is for our wisdom, our glory and most importantly for the defeat of Satan and his cohorts in the kingdom of darkness. This fact is the basis of the whole chapter two of first Corinthians.

[1] *And when I came to you, brothers and sisters, proclaiming to you the testimony of God [concerning salvation through Christ], I did not come with superiority of speech or of wisdom [no lofty words of eloquence or of philosophy as a Greek orator might do];*
[2] *for I made the decision to know nothing [that is, to forego philosophical or theological discussions regarding inconsequential things and opinions while] among you except Jesus Christ, and Him crucified [and the meaning of His redemptive, substitutionary death and His resurrection].*
[3] *I came to you in [a state of] weakness and fear and great trembling.*
[4] *And my message and my preaching were not in persuasive words of wisdom [using clever rhetoric], but [they were delivered] in demonstration of the [Holy] Spirit [operating through me] and of [His] power [stirring the minds of the listeners and persuading them],*
[5] *so that your faith would not rest on the wisdom and rhetoric of men, but on the power of God.*
[6] *Yet we do speak wisdom among those spiritually mature [believers who have teachable hearts and a greater understanding]; but*

[it is a higher] wisdom not [the wisdom] of this present age nor of the rulers and leaders of this age, who are passing away;
[7] *but we speak God's wisdom in a mystery, the wisdom once hidden [from man, but now revealed to us by God, that wisdom] which God predestined before the ages to our glory [to lift us into the glory of His presence].*
[8] *None of the rulers of this age recognized and understood this wisdom; for if they had, they would not have crucified the Lord of glory;*
[9] *but just as it is written [in Scripture], "THINGS WHICH THE EYE HAS NOT SEEN AND THE EAR HAS NOT HEARD, AND WHICH HAVE NOT ENTERED THE HEART OF MAN, ALL THAT GOD HAS PREPARED FOR THOSE WHO LOVE HIM [who hold Him in affectionate reverence, who obey Him, and who gratefully recognize the benefits that He has bestowed]."*
[10] *For God has unveiled them and revealed them to us through the [Holy] Spirit; for the Spirit searches all things [diligently], even [sounding and measuring] the [profound] depths of God [the divine counsels and things far beyond human*

understanding].
11 *For what person knows the thoughts and motives of a man except the man's spirit within him? So also no one knows the thoughts of God except the Spirit of God.*
12 *Now we have received, not the spirit of the world, but the [Holy] Spirit who is from God, so that we may know and understand the [wonderful] things freely given to us by God.*
13 *We also speak of these things, not in words taught or supplied by human wisdom, but in those taught by the Spirit, combining and interpreting spiritual thoughts with spiritual words [for those being guided by the Holy Spirit].*
14 *But the natural [unbelieving] man does not accept the things [the teachings and revelations] of the Spirit of God, for they are foolishness [absurd and illogical] to him; and he is incapable of understanding them, because they are spiritually discerned and appreciated, [and he is unqualified to judge spiritual matters].*
15 *But the spiritual man [the spiritually mature Christian] judges all things [questions, examines and applies what the Holy Spirit reveals], yet is himself judged by no one [the unbeliever cannot judge and*

> *understand the believer's spiritual nature].*
> [16] *For WHO HAS KNOWN THE MIND and PURPOSES OF THE LORD, SO AS TO INSTRUCT HIM? But we have the mind of Christ [to be guided by His thoughts and purposes].*
> **1 Corinthians 2:1-16 AMP**

The Apostle Paul alluded to this fact that Jesus was made a sin offering, crucified on the Calvary Altar to pay the penalty for the sin of the world that we might become the righteousness of God in Christ.

> [21] *For God made Christ, who never sinned, to be the offering for our sin, so that we could be made right with God through Christ.*
> **2 Corinthians 5:21 NLT**

It will be worthwhile at this point to look at the definition of an 'ALTAR'.

An altar is described as a structure on which offerings are made to a deity. The Hebrew word for altar is "Mizbeah," which means to slaughter or place of slaughter.

In Greek it is rendered as "thusiasterion," 'a place of sacrifice'.

What makes an ALTAR very important can be attributed to the fact that it sanctifies whatever is placed upon it. This fact was expounded and revealed by Jesus Himself to expose the foolishness of the Pharisee and scribes about their lack of understanding of the significance of the altar, even from the Old Testament perspective.

> 15 *Woe unto you, scribes and Pharisees, hypocrites! for ye compass sea and land to make one proselyte, and when he is made, ye make him twofold more the child of hell than yourselves.*
> 16 *Woe unto you, ye blind guides, which say, Whosoever shall swear by the temple, it is nothing; but whosoever shall swear by the gold of the temple, he is a debtor!*
> 17 *Ye fools and blind: for whether is greater, the gold, or the temple that sanctifieth the gold?*
> 18 *And, Whosoever shall swear by the altar, it is nothing; but whosoever sweareth by the gift that is upon it, he is guilty.*
> 19 *Ye fools and blind: for whether is greater, the gift, or the altar that sanctifieth the gift?*
> 20 *Whoso therefore shall swear by the altar, sweareth by it, and by all things thereon.*
> **Matthew 23:15-20**

This shows that both Jesus as sacrificial offering and the cross of calvary are equally important.

5

THE MYSTERY OF THE CROSS AS THE PROVERBIAL KEY OF THE HOUSE OF DAVID UPON JESUS' SHOULDER

Through the foolishness of the cross, Jesus became our wisdom making it easy for believers to be in the perfect will of God. Believers therefore have been enjoined to follow the humility of Christ in submitting to the perfect will of God. The passage below symbolically and prophetically revealed the hidden wisdom of God, which will be fulfilled in the New Testament. In this revelation, we see Jesus carrying the cross upon his shoulder in which the cross becomes the key of the house of David, thereby facilitating the access to God's presence (Holies of Holies).

The cross is the key that opened the life gate that was shut against humanity as a result of the sin of Adam and Eve.

There are two prophetic allegories that

foreshadowed Jesus carrying the cross on his shoulder to the Calvary. The first allegory was when Isaac carried the wood on his shoulder upon which he was to be sacrificed by his father, Abraham.

> [6] *Then Abraham took the wood for the burnt offering and laid it on [the shoulders of] Isaac his son, and he took the fire (firepot) in his own hand and the [sacrificial] knife; and the two of them walked on together.*
> [7] *And Isaac said to Abraham, "My father!" And he said, "Here I am, my son." Isaac said, "Look, the fire and the wood, but where is the lamb for the burnt offering?"*
> [8] *Abraham said, "My son, God will provide for Himself a lamb for the burnt offering." So the two walked on together.*
> [9] *When they came to the place of which God had told him, Abraham built an altar there and arranged the wood, and bound Isaac his son and placed him on the altar, on top of the wood.*
> **Genesis 22:6-9 AMP**

History confirmed that Isaac and Abraham arrived at a mountain known as Calvary (Mount Moriah), which is one of the mountains that surround Jerusalem.

The second prophetic allegory about Jesus carrying the cross on His shoulder is the passage below, a prophecy about king Eliakim:

> [20] *And it shall come to pass in that day, that I will call my servant Eliakim the son of Hilkiah:*
> [21] *And I will clothe him with thy robe, and strengthen him with thy girdle, and I will commit thy government into his hand: and he shall be a father to the inhabitants of Jerusalem, and to the house of Judah.*
> [22] *And the key of the house of David will I lay upon his shoulder; so he shall open, and none shall shut; and he shall shut, and none shall open.*
> **Isaiah 22:20-22**

> [6] *For unto us a child is born, unto us a son is given: and the government shall be upon his shoulder: and his name shall be called Wonderful, Counsellor, The mighty God, The everlasting Father, The Prince of Peace.*
> [7] *Of the increase of his government and peace there shall be no end, upon the throne of David, and upon his kingdom, to order it, and to establish it with judgment and*

with justice from henceforth even for ever.
The zeal of the LORD of hosts will perform this.
Isaiah 9:6-7

We need to critically examine these prophecies in parallel and consider how they relate to Christ the Messiah carrying the cross upon His shoulder to Calvary. The Bible mentioned that these two characters, Eliakim and Christ, will be rulers, because they were chosen by God at a specific time and dispensation to fulfil God's purpose, and both directly from the lineage of David. The name Eliakim, in Hebrew, means "God raised," "God established," or "raised by God."

The Tenfold Exaltation Of Eliakim Foreshadowing Christ As King

The prophecy in Isaiah 22 revealed a tenfold exaltation of Eliakim, which I believe figuratively mirrors Jesus Christ, who was to come 700 years later through the same lineage of Eliakim, one of the highly exalted ancient King of Judah (Luke 3:30).

1. I will call him (vs 20).
2. I will clothe him (vs 21).
3. I will strengthen him (vs 21).
4. I will commit the government to him (vs 21).
5. He shall be a father to the inhabitants of Jerusalem and to the house of Judah (vs 21).

6. I will give him the key of David (vs 22). In my opinion, I believe this is the calvary cross.
7. He shall have authority to open and shut and none shall hinder him (vs 22). This was confirmed in Philippians 2:2-11, Jesus having authority in the heaven, on the earth and underneath the earth.
8. I will make him permanent (vs 23). Jesus as a seated King forever.
9. He shall be exalted to his father's house (vs 23).
10. He shall have all the glory of his father's house (vs 24). This points to the reconciliation of man and restoration of all wealth and the riches of this world that have been stolen by Satan from Adam (Colossians 1:20-22).

Isaiah 22:22 is very symbolic and proverbial in content, and I believe Jesus fits into the description of the exaltation of Eliakim

.Unsurprisingly, King Eliakim was mentioned in the genealogy of Jesus Christ (Luke 3:30). As a descendant of king Eliakim, He fulfilled the Messianic part of the prophecy.

The Key of David

A crucial part of these prophecies is the phrase "the key of the house of David," which God would lay upon Christ's shoulder.

> [22] *And the key of the house of David will I lay upon his shoulder; so he shall open, and none shall shut; and he shall shut and none shall open.*
> **Isaiah 22:22**

The Bible ascribes this statement to Jesus alone according to the scriptures below:

> [18] *I am the Living One; I was dead, and now look, I am alive for ever and ever! And I hold the keys of death and Hades.*
> **Revelation 1:18**

> [7] *To the angel of the church in Philadelphia write: These are the words of him who is holy and true, who holds the key of David. What he opens no one can shut, and what he shuts no one can open.*
> **Revelation 3:7**

The question is, how can a "key" be carried upon one's shoulder? According to oriental (Eastern) culture, keys were usually large and often carried on the shoulder of wealthy people and people of authority. The possession of a key was evidence of AUTHORITY, TRUST, ACCESS, OR POSSESSION OF WEALTH/PROPERTY. The word key, therefore, represented access and authority.

Symbolically, according to the context of Isaiah 22:22, this confirms Isaiah 9:6-7 which states that the key to the governmental dominion authority will be upon Christ's shoulder.

> [6] *For unto us a child is born, unto us a son is given: and the government shall be upon his shoulder: and his name shall be called Wonderful, Counsellor, The mighty God, The everlasting Father, The Prince of Peace.*
> [7] *Of the increase of his government and peace there shall be no end, upon the throne of David, and upon his kingdom, to order it, and to establish it with judgment and with justice from henceforth even for ever. The zeal of the LORD of hosts will perform this.*
> **Isaiah 9:6,7**

No wonder Jesus enjoined His disciples that the only attestation to their calling as the Apostles of Jesus was their readiness to carry the message of the cross, which represented the revelation about the totality of the finished work of redemption of which His crucifixion is the precursor. That is to say that the metamorphosis (the process) of the redemption of man originated from what began on the cross...

crucifixion, burial, resurrection, ascension and glorification (seated and being enthroned).

I believe the first key of the kingdom that Jesus promised is that of the revelation of the redemptive power in the blood and the sanctifying power of the cross. I am also realising as I am learning from the Holy Spirit that there are certain realms of revelation you cannot be exposed to, certain realms of glory and power that one cannot attain, until you have certain understanding of the mystery of the keys of the kingdom relating to the mystery of the blood and the cross. Jesus promised His Ecclesia that He will give us the keys of the kingdom of heaven, and I believe the revelation of the message and the mystery of the cross is the number one key.

> 19 *I will give you the keys of the kingdom of heaven; whatever you bind on earth will be bound in heaven, and whatever you loose on earth will be loosed in heaven.* **Matthew 16:19 NIV**

6

FIVETEEN REVELATIONS ON HOW THE CALVARY CROSS FACILITATED THE PROCESS OF HUMAN REDEMPTION

"A wooden key is not so beautiful as a golden one, but if it can open the door when the golden one cannot, it is far more useful" (St Augustine).

> [22] *And the key of the house of David I will lay upon his shoulder; he shall open and no one shall shut, he shall shut and no one shall open.*
>
> **Isaiah 22:22 AMPC**

As the Holy Spirit incubated the message of this book within me, He gave me fifteen significant reasons why the message of the Cross should be given utmost priority in our pulpit at this critical point in the history of the Church. The scriptures declare that "The secret things belong to the LORD our God, but the things revealed belong to us and to our sons forever, that we may observe all the words of this law" (Deuteronomy 29:29 NASB).

A mystery is defined as "something that is difficult or impossible to understand or explain." In Biblical Greek, the term refers to "that which awaits disclosure or interpretation." It is also a "secret hidden in God, which can never be known unless revealed by God." This chapter will focus on highlighting some powerful revelations about the power of Calvary Cross and demonstrate how it achieved God's purpose in the salvation of man and reconciliation of all that Satan stole from Adam.

Revelation #1: The Cross unlocked the gate of paradise (Garden of Eden) that was locked against humanity after the sin of Adam (Genesis 3:22-24; Hebrew 10:19-23).

Revelation #2: The cross in the New Testament represents the tree of life from where God's abundant life flows. This was the tree God refused Adam and Eve to partake from before they were sent out of the Garden of Eden. The Cross, therefore, became the tree of abundant life which is now made available to man (Genesis 3:22; Zechariah 13:1-2; John 10:10, 6:53-57).

Revelation #3: The believers' new creation covenant realities were achieved through the extraordinary strategy of the power of the Cross (Genesis 2:21-14; Matthew 27:45-50; John 19:34; Ephesians 2:5-10).

Revelation #4: The cross is not an ordinary tree, but the supernatural altar where the blood of Jesus was shed to sprinkle the nations as the ultimate price for the salvation of humanity (John 19:33-34; Isaiah 52:15).

Revelation #5: The Calvary Cross was the mountain from where the fountain of the blood of Jesus flows for the cleansing of sins and iniquity (Zechariah 13:1-2).

Revelation #6: Calvary Cross was the key that Isaiah prophesised that it will be laid upon the shoulder of Jesus (Isaiah 22:22, John 19:16-17: Revelation 1:18).

Revelation #7: Calvary tree is the key that opened the gates of Death and Hades to set the captives free from the dominion of Satan and declare His victory over hell and death (John 12:30-33; Colossians 1:12-14; Revelation 1:18).

Revelation #8: Jesus hung on the Calvary Cross as a "scapegoat" to atone for the sins of the world and bear all our curses, thereby securing for us the Abrahams covenant of abundant blessings (Galatians 3:13-14; Isaiah 53:4; John 1:29).

Revelation #9: The tree of death (the tree of knowledge of good and evil) was exchanged with the tree of eternal life and salvation which is Calvary Cross (John 10:10, 6:53-56, 15:1-6).

Revelation #10: Through the Calvary Cross, the fruit of the tree of the knowledge of good and evil was exchanged for the fruit of eternal life, truth and righteousness, Jesus being the first fruit of the tree of life (1 Corinthians 15:20-23; John15:1-4).

Revelation #11: One of the most significant truths about the mystery of the cross is that the problem of man started in the garden of Eden when Adam ate from the tree of disobedience; in the same way, Calvary Cross became the tree of obedience which Jesus Christ endured, thereby bringing solution to Adam's sin of disobedience (Genesis 3:1-12; Matthew 27:50-53; Philippians 2:8; Colossians 2:13-15).

Revelation #12: The power of the cross carries the supernatural capacity to save and sanctify mankind, and to draw humanity back to God (John 12:32-33; Exodus 29:42-45; Matthew 23:19-21).

Revelation #13: It was on the cross that Jesus defeated Satan and terminated his dominion, authority and works on the earth (Mark 27:45-46,51; Colossians 2:13-15).

Revelation #14: We were crucified and died with Christ on the cross to become new creatures in Him (2 Corinthians 5:15-17; Galatians 2:20). This is exactly what God did when He put Adam to sleep to create Eve from him as a "new creation" (Genesis 2:18,21-25).

Revelation #15: The tree of the knowledge of good and evil put the curse of Ichabod (the loss of God's glory and presence) upon humanity, but the Calvary cross restored our access to God's presence and glory (Hebrews 10:19-21; Colossians 1:20-22; Genesis 3:1-9).

Revelation #16: On the cross of Calvary our sins were cleansed, and we were presented to God as blameless (Ephesians 2:13-15).

The eternal plan of God for humanity was sabotaged in the Garden of Eden when Adam and Eve fell into sin of disobedience by eating the forbidden tree. This, however, did not mean that the original eternal plan of God for man was defeated, because the Lamb of God had already been "slain from the foundation of the world" (Revelation 13:8). God, at His set time, about 4000 years after man's disobedience, God turned the situation around. This happened through the obedience of Jesus Christ to go through the painful death on the cross. This act of obedience restored the status of man as king and priest over the earth, while Jesus is the High Priest and the King of Kings.

> [8] *Now when He had taken the scroll, the four living creatures and the twenty-four elders fell down before the Lamb, each having a harp, and golden bowls full of incense, which are the prayers of the saints.*
> [9] *And they sang a new song, saying: "You are worthy to take the scroll, And to open its seals; For You were slain, And have redeemed us to God by Your blood Out of every tribe and tongue and people and nation,*
> [10] *And have made us kings and priests to our God; And we shall reign on the earth.*
> **Revelation 5:8-10 NKJV**

Hallelujah!

7
CALVARY CROSS AS THE TREE OF LIFE

The last three verses of Genesis 3 are very vital to the understanding of the eternal plan of God for human redemption after Adam and Eve lost the first Paradise. The judgment that God passed upon Adam and Eve was that they will no more have access to the tree of life and for this reason God sent them out of the Garden of Eden. However, to facilitate redemption and reconciliation of man, God had eternally prepared another "tree of life," the Calvary Cross, with Jesus as the first fruit of the tree.

> 22 *And the LORD God said, Behold, the man is become as one of us, to know good and evil: and now, lest he put forth his hand, and take also of the tree of life, and eat, and live for ever:*

> [23] *Therefore the LORD God sent him forth from the garden of Eden, to till the ground from whence he was taken.*
> **Genesis 3:22-23**

Furthermore, in order that man would not dare to come back to the garden to partake of the fruit of the tree of life, God shut the gates and made it permanently inaccessible by stationing angelic hosts (Cherubim) to guard and keep the entrance with flaming swords, turning every way.

> [24] *So he drove out the man; and he placed at the east of the garden of Eden Cherubims, and a flaming sword which turned every way, to keep the way of the tree of life.*
> Genesis 3:24

Significance Of The Tree Of Life And Its Fruit

I believe access to the tree of life and its fruit opens the life gate to eternity - to God's glory, presence, and unlimited power. However, even though God had forbidden Adam and Eve to partake from the tree in the Garden of Eden, He already made provision for another tree of life through His eternal plan and purpose. The Cross of calvary is the altar predestined to facilitate a once-and-for-all sacrifice for the redemption and the reconciliation between God and man.

Essentially, God had prepared a new and better way, a new gate with a new key, to gain access to Paradise, the citadel of eternal life and God's presence. This new way is facilitated by the blood and the cross of Calvary. Jesus, indeed, became the fruit of the tree of life. Jesus Himself made the following statement to corroborate this mystery in the following passages:

> 14 *And as Moses lifted up the serpent in the wilderness, even so must the Son of man be lifted up (on the Calvary Cross, the tree of life... paraphrased)*
> 15 *That whosoever believeth in him should not perish, but have eternal life.*
> 16 *For God so loved the world, that he gave his only begotten Son, that whosoever believeth in him should not perish, but have everlasting life.*
> **John 3:14-16**

> 32 *And I, if I be lifted up from the earth, will draw all men unto me. This he said, signifying what death he should die.*
> **John 12:32**

Jesus made it clear in the above statement that once He is lifted up from the earth and hanged on the Calvary Cross, He will restore all men back to God.

In this profound statement, Jesus described how He will fully restore what we lost after Adam and Eve were sent out of the Garden of Eden (paradise, freedom, and eternal life). This fact is further highlighted in the following passage:

> 6 *Jesus saith unto him, I am the way, the truth, and the life: no man cometh unto the Father, but by me.*
> **John 14:6**

We can break this statement into three main phrases:

- *I am the way…* leading humanity back to paradise through the gate that was once shut but now open (Genesis 3:22-24). The cross of calvary, soaked in the blood, became the key of David that opened the life gate to God's presence. Hallelujah!
- *I am the truth…* challenging and overcoming the lie and deception of Satan that made Adam and Eve to disobey God (Genesis 3:1-6).
- *I am the life…* Jesus is now the way back to the abundant, eternal life of God which Adam and Eve were forbidden to partake of (Genesis 3:22-23).

The above statements help us understand what Jesus did to destroy the works of the devil.

[8] He that committeth sin is of the devil; for the devil sinneth from the beginning. For this purpose the Son of God was manifested, that he might destroy the works of the devil.

1 John 3:8

Over 2000 years ago, the tree of life and the first fruit of life was displayed in Jerusalem when Jesus hung on the Calvary cross to consummate the eternal plan of God for man's redemption. This phenomenon fulfilled Christ's own statement that when He is lifted up from the earth, He will draw all men to God and to Himself.

[31] "Now is the judgment of this world; now the ruler of this world will be cast out.
[32] And I, if I am lifted up from the earth, will draw all peoples to Myself."
[33] This He said, signifying by what death He would die.

John 12:31-33 NKJV

The passage below is the consummation of God's eternal plan to save humanity.

[45] Now from the sixth hour there was darkness over all the land unto the ninth hour.

*46 And about the ninth hour Jesus cried
with a loud voice, saying, Eli, Eli, lama
sabachthani? that is to say, My God, my
God, why hast thou forsaken me?*
*47 Some of them that stood there, when they
heard that, said, This man calleth for Elias.*
*48 And straightway one of them ran, and
took a spunge, and filled it with vinegar,
and put it on a reed, and gave him to drink.*
*49 The rest said, Let be, let us see whether
Elias will come to save him.*
*50 Jesus, when he had cried again with a
loud voice, yielded up the ghost.*
*51 And, behold, the veil of the temple was
rent in twain from the top to the bottom;
and the earth did quake, and the rocks rent;*
*52 And the graves were opened; and many
bodies of the saints which slept arose,*
*53 And came out of the graves after his
resurrection, and went into the holy city,
and appeared unto many.*
Matthew 27:45-53

On this very day, the access to Paradise was given back to man to demonstrate the power of God's saving grace by the blood of His Cross. By this grace, an armed robber was saved on the cross with the assurance of walking with Jesus to the paradise on that very same day that he was saved on the cross.

41 And we indeed justly; for we receive the due reward of our deeds: but this man hath done nothing amiss.
42 And he said unto Jesus, Lord, remember me when thou comest into thy kingdom.
43 And Jesus said unto him, Verily I say unto thee, Today shalt thou be with me in paradise.
Luke 23:42-43

Jesus destroyed all the works of Satan through His crucifixion, death, burial and resurrection. He conquered the power of death and reconciled humanity back to God. On the very day that Jesus was crucified, the power of grave was conquered, corruption was conquered, and resurrection power manifested to take over the gate of hell. The dead were raised and came back to life.

50 And when Jesus had cried out again in a loud voice, he gave up his spirit.
51 At that moment the curtain of the temple was torn in two from top to bottom. The earth shook, the rocks split
52 and the tombs broke open. The bodies of many holy people who had died were raised to life.
53 They came out of the tombs after Jesus'

resurrection and went into the holy city and appeared to many people.
Matthew 27:50-53 NIV

[19] *For it pleased the Father that in Him all the fullness should dwell,*
[20] *and by Him to reconcile all things to Himself, by Him, whether things on earth or things in heaven, having made peace through the blood of His cross.*
[21] *And you, who once were alienated and enemies in your mind by wicked works, yet now He has reconciled.*
Colossians 1:19-21

The onus is now upon the Ecclesia to enforce the victory Jesus won on the cross and walk in the authority He gave to us as He has ascended into heaven. May God give us wisdom and grace to diligently pay attention to the Great commission. Amen!

To God be the glory
By Fanny Crosby

1. To God be the glory, great things he hath done!
So loved he the world that he gave us his Son,
who yielded his life an atonement for sin,
and opened the lifegate that all may go in.

Refrain
Praise the Lord, praise the Lord,
let the earth hear his voice!
Praise the Lord, praise the Lord,
let the people rejoice!
O come to the Father through Jesus the Son,
and give him the glory, great things he hath done!

2. O perfect redemption, the purchase of blood,
to every believer the promise of God;
the vilest offender who truly believes,
that moment from Jesus a pardon receives.

8

THE SIGNIFICANCE OF JESUS CARRYING THE CROSS TO CALVARY

There were many processes involved in the redemption of man in relation to what happened to Jesus right from the time of His arrest to resurrection day. One of these was the carrying of the cross on His shoulder to Calvary. This was prophesied about seven hundred years before Jesus came into the world.

> 22 *The key of the house of David I will lay on his shoulder; so he shall open, and no one shall shut; And he shall shut, and no one shall open.*
> **Isaiah 22:22**

Over 2,000 years ago, on his way to Calvary, the key of the house of David was laid upon Christ's shoulder and it is through this key that access to God's presence was secured.

> [16] *Then delivered he him therefore unto them to be crucified. And they took Jesus, and led him away.*
> [17] *And he bearing his cross went forth into a place called the place of a skull, which is called in the Hebrew Golgotha:*
> [18] *Where they crucified him, and two other with him, on either side one, and Jesus in the midst.*
> [19] *And Pilate wrote a title, and put it on the cross. And the writing was JESUS OF NAZARETH THE KING OF THE JEWS.*
> **John 19:16-19**

The Cross on the shoulder of Jesus was very important. It represented the altar upon which the sacrifice would be slaughtered. Secondly, the altar is significant to the sacrifice that will be performed on it.

In the passage, we see Jesus carrying the altar where His life will be offered as a sacrificial offering for the sins of the world. The mystery of the significance of the altar is that it is the altar that sanctifies the offering placed on it. Thus, the Cross carried the sanctifying power of the Body of Christ that was laid on it.

> [19] *You blind men! Which is greater: the gift, or the altar which makes the gift sacred?*
> [20] *So whoever swears by the altar swears by it and by everything on it.*
> **Matthew 23:19-20 AMPC**

God made Jesus a sacrificial offering for our sins that we may become the righteousness of God in Him. Christ never sinned, but God treated him as a sinner, so Christ could make us acceptable to God.

> [21] *For God made Christ, who never sinned, to be the offering for our sin, so that we could be made right with God through Christ.*
> **2 Corinthians 5:21 NLT**

When they put the cross upon the shoulder of JESUS, thinking that they were punishing him, little did they know that they were fulfilling the written prophecy that God would put the key of the house of David (the church of God and her authority) upon Christ' shoulder.

> [22] *The key of the house of David I will lay on his shoulder; so he shall open, and no one shall shut; And he shall shut, and no one shall open.*
> **Isaiah 22:22 NKJV**

This is the "mystery key" that will open the life gate to give access to God's presence, thereby reconciling humanity back to God. Out of this mystery will come the power of God for the salvation of men. The fulfilment of the above prophecy became the revelation of the mystery of the cross, giving access to the Holy of Holies in God's presence.

> [19] *Therefore, brethren, having boldness to enter the Holiest by the blood of Jesus,*
> [20] *by a new and living way which He consecrated for us, through the veil, that is, His flesh,*
> [21] *and having a High Priest over the house of God,*
> [22] *let us draw near with a true heart in full assurance of faith, having our hearts sprinkled from an evil conscience and our bodies washed with pure water.*
> **Hebrews 10:19-22 NKJV**

> [7] *And to the angel of the church in Philadelphia write, 'These things says He who is holy, He who is true, "He who has the key of David, He who opens and no one shuts, and shuts and no one opens."*
> **Revelation 3:7 NKJV**

This is what Paul described as the mystery and the foolishness of the cross:

> [18] *For the message of the cross is foolishness to those who are perishing, but to us who are being saved it is the power of God.*
> **1 Corinthians 1:18**

About 4,000 years before Jesus came to this world, the door to the life gate (Paradise) was shut to humanity because of the disobedience of Adam and Eve when they ate the forbidden fruit. Thus, both were lost from the unbroken presence of God the Father; they became naked and hid themselves because the glory of God had departed from them.

> [1] *Now the serpent was more crafty than any of the wild animals the LORD God had made. He said to the woman, "Did God really say, 'You must not eat from any tree in the garden'?"*
> [2] *The woman said to the serpent, "We may eat fruit from the trees in the garden,*
> [3] *but God did say, 'You must not eat fruit from the tree that is in the middle of the garden, and you must not touch it, or you will die.'"*
> [4] *"You will not certainly die," the serpent said to the woman.*
> [5] *"For God knows that when you eat from it*

your eyes will be opened, and you will be like God, knowing good and evil."
6 *When the woman saw that the fruit of the tree was good for food and pleasing to the eye, and also desirable for gaining wisdom, she took some and ate it. She also gave some to her husband, who was with her, and he ate it.*
7 *Then the eyes of both of them were opened, and they realized they were naked; so they sewed fig leaves together and made coverings for themselves.*
8 *Then the man and his wife heard the sound of the LORD God as he was walking in the garden in the cool of the day, and they hid from the LORD God among the trees of the garden.*
9 *But the LORD God called to the man, "Where are you?"*
10 *He answered, "I heard you in the garden, and I was afraid because I was naked; so I hid."*
Genesis 3:1-10 NIV

As a result of their sin, the gate to eternal life was shut and angel was placed at the gate to eternal life to prevent man from accessing the tree of the fruit of eternal life.

[22] *And the LORD God said, Behold, the man is become as one of us, to know good and evil: and now, lest he put forth his hand, and take also of the tree of life, and eat, and live for ever:*
[23] *Therefore the LORD God sent him forth from the garden of Eden, to till the ground) from whence he was taken.*
[24] *So he drove out the man; and he placed at the east of the garden of Eden Cherubims, and a flaming sword which turned every way, to keep the way of the tree of life.*
Genesis 3:22-24

But over 2000 years ago, Jesus was lifted up on the cross and crucified to secure redemption and reconciliation for man.

[50] *And Jesus cried out again with a loud voice, and yielded up His spirit.*
[51] *Then, behold, the veil of the temple was torn in two from top to bottom; and the earth quaked, and the rocks were split,*
[52] *and the graves were opened; and many bodies of the saints who had fallen asleep were raised;*
[53] *and coming out of the graves after His resurrection, they went into the holy city and appeared to many.*
Matthew 27:50-53 NKJV

> 28 *After this, Jesus, knowing that all things*
> *were now accomplished, that the Scripture*
> *might be fulfilled, said, "I thirst!"*
> 29 *Now a vessel full of sour wine was sitting*
> *there; and they filled a sponge with sour*
> *wine, put it on hyssop, and put it to His*
> *mouth.*
> 30 *So when Jesus had received the sour*
> *wine, He said, "It is finished!" And bowing*
> *His head, He gave up His spirit.*
> **John 19:28-30 NKJV**

We can see that the gate of eternal life was opened simultaneously the gate of death and hell was shut as Jesus shed His blood on the cross. In fact, the passage above said that the grave opened and the dead in them came out in full view of onlookers. Hallelujah!

9

THE CROSS AS A SYMBOL OF CHURCH DOMINION POWER AND AUTHORITY

Jesus expects us to preach and affirm the authority of the power of the CROSS daily. This is one of the reasons why He charged His disciples to carry their cross daily and follow Him. When we preach about the power of the cross and the blood on daily basis, we are reminding Satan where he lost his authority and power. Hence, every Christian message must reflect and centre around the power of the CROSS.

In other words, the thrust (the pillar) of our commission is meant to be the message of the cross – the crucifixion, burial, and resurrection of the Lord Jesus Christ. This must be our daily message and we should not be ashamed of preaching it, neither should we fall into the temptation of avoiding the centrality of the cross.

[21] *From that time forth began Jesus to shew unto his disciples, how that he must go unto Jerusalem, and suffer many things of the elders and chief priests and scribes, and be killed, and be raised again the third day.*
[22] *Then Peter took him, and began to rebuke him, saying, Be it far from thee, Lord: this shall not be unto thee.*
[23] *But he turned, and said unto Peter, Get thee behind me, Satan: thou art an offence unto me: for thou savourest not the things that be of God, but those that be of men.*
[24] *Then said Jesus unto his disciples, If any man will come after me, let him deny himself, and take up his cross, and follow me.*
Matthew 16:21-24

[38] *And he that taketh not his cross, and followeth after me, is not worthy of me.*
Matthew 10:38

Jesus told His disciples to preach the cross daily even if it made them look foolish before the religious leaders of their time, because the power of the cross would facilitate the release and manifestation of the wisdom of God; the cross would turn the wisdom of the prince of this world (Satan) into foolishness.

18 *The message of the cross is foolish to those
who are headed for destruction! But we
who are being saved know it is the very
power of God.*
19 *As the Scriptures say, "I will destroy the
wisdom of the wise and discard the
intelligence of the intelligent."*
20 *So where does this leave the philosophers,
the scholars, and the world's brilliant
debaters? God has made the wisdom of this
world look foolish.*
21 *Since God in his wisdom saw to it that the
world would never know him through
human wisdom, he has used our foolish
preaching to save those who believe.*
22 *It is foolish to the Jews, who ask for signs
from heaven. And it is foolish to the Greeks,
who seek human wisdom.*
23 *So when we preach that Christ was
crucified, the Jews are offended and the
Gentiles say it's all nonsense.*
24 *But to those called by God to salvation,
both Jews and Gentiles, Christ is the power
of God and the wisdom of God.*
25 *This foolish plan of God is wiser than the
wisest of human plans, and God's
weakness is stronger than the greatest of
human strength.*
26 *Remember, dear brothers and sisters, that
few of you were wise in the world's eyes or*

powerful or wealthy when God called you.
[27] *Instead, God chose things the world considers foolish in order to shame those who think they are wise. And he chose things that are powerless to shame those who are powerful.*
[28] *God chose things despised by the world, things counted as nothing at all, and used them to bring to nothing what the world considers important.*
[29] *As a result, no one can ever boast in the presence of God.*
[30] *God has united you with Christ Jesus. For our benefit God made him to be wisdom itself. Christ made us right with God; he made us pure and holy, and he freed us from sin.*
[31] *Therefore, as the Scriptures say, "If you want to boast, boast only about the LORD."*
1 Corinthians 1:18-31 NLT

The cross of Jesus represents the key to securing our redemptive power and authority. The preaching of the cross must, therefore, be the epicentre of our message, because it is the key that unlocks the life gate leading to paradise; the ultimate price for the sins of all humanity was paid on the cross, securing the salvation for all mankind. This is the basis of the great commission and the good news which reveals the agape love of God towards mankind.

Jesus Himself affirmed that He will be lifted and crucified on the cross to secure salvation for mankind, and this would demonstrate God's agape love.

> 14 *Just as Moses lifted up the [bronze] serpent in the desert [on a pole], so must the Son of Man be lifted up [on the cross],*
> 15 *so that whoever believes will in Him have eternal life [after physical death, and will actually live forever].*
> 16 *"For God so [greatly] loved and dearly prized the world, that He [even] gave His [One and] only begotten Son, so that whoever believes and trusts in Him [as Savior] shall not perish, but have eternal life.*
> 17 *For God did not send the Son into the world to judge and condemn the world [that is, to initiate the final judgment of the world], but that the world might be saved through Him.*
> 18 *Whoever believes and has decided to trust in Him [as personal Savior and Lord] is not judged [for this one, there is no judgment, no rejection, no condemnation]; but the one who does not believe [and has decided to reject Him as personal Savior and Lord]*

is judged already [that one has been convicted and sentenced], because he has not believed and trusted in the name of the [One and] only begotten Son of God [the One who is truly unique, the only One of His kind, the One who alone can save him].
[19] *This is the judgment [that is, the cause for indictment, the test by which people are judged, the basis for the sentence]: the Light has come into the world, and people loved the darkness rather than the Light, for their deeds were evil.*
John 3:14-19 AMP

[13] *Greater love hath no man than this, that a man lay down his life for his friends.*
John 15:13

Jesus charged His disciples to live daily by the revelation of the mystery of the power of the cross. In the same way, Apostle Paul encouraged the believers to focus on the power of the cross where Jesus was crucified.

[1] *And I, brethren, when I came to you, did not come with excellence of speech or of wisdom declaring to you the testimony of God.*
[2] *For I determined not to know anything*

among you except Jesus Christ and Him crucified.
1 Corinthians 2:1-2 NKJV

The reason why Paul insisted that the only thing he would like the Corinthian brethren to know was the fact that the cross was the central message of salvation. It was the most powerful key of the kingdom of heaven, by which they could gain access to God's presence.

22 *And the LORD God said, Behold, the man is become as one of us, to know good and evil: and now, lest he put forth his hand, and take also of the tree of life, and eat, and live for ever:*
23 *Therefore the LORD God sent him forth from the garden of Eden, to till the ground from whence he was taken.*
24 *So he drove out the man; and he placed at the east of the garden of Eden Cherubims, and a flaming sword which turned every way, to keep the way of the tree of life.*
Genesis 3:22-24

When Jesus Christ was suspended on the cross, a Roman Soldier pierced through His side with a sword, and blood and water gushed out. By this act, God opened the life gate and removed the angel placed at the gate of paradise to chase man away from God's presence.

> [34] *But one of the soldiers with a spear pierced his side, and forthwith came there out blood and water.*
> **John 19:34**

When this happened, the veil that shielded the holy of holies rented from top to bottom (Mark 15:37-38), and access to God's presence was made available to as many as would believe in Jesus.

> [19] *Having therefore, brethren, boldness to enter into the holiest by the blood of Jesus,*
> [20] *By a new and living way, which he hath consecrated for us, through the veil, that is to say, his flesh.*
> **Hebrews 10:19-20**

We praise God for the free flow of the fountain of blood and water that came forth from Jesus' side when He hung on the cross of Calvary. Indeed, the power in the blood gave us access to God's presence as indicated in the above passage.

10
THE APOSTLE PAUL'S BOASTING ABOUT THE CROSS EXPLAINED

In this chapter, I want to highlight a few passages in the Bible that underscore the reason why Apostle Paul always boasted about the mystery of the cross. I believe that we, the church of Jesus Christ, must not do any less.

> [18] *For the preaching of the cross is to them that perish foolishness; but unto us which are saved it is the power of God.*
> **1 Corinthians 1:18**

> [12] *Those who want to make a good impression and a fine show in the flesh would try to compel you to receive circumcision, simply so that they may escape being persecuted for allegiance to*

the cross of Christ (the Messiah, the Anointed One).
13 *For even the circumcised [Jews] themselves do not [really] keep the Law, but they want to have you circumcised in order that they may glory in your flesh (your subjection to external rites).*
14 *But far be it from me to glory [in anything or anyone] except in the cross of our Lord Jesus Christ (the Messiah) through Whom the world has been crucified to me, and I to the world!*
15 *For neither is circumcision [now] of any importance, nor uncircumcision, but [only] a new creation [the result of a new birth and a new nature in Christ Jesus, the Messiah].*
Galatians 6:12-15 AMPC

1 *When I first came to you, dear brothers and sisters, I didn't use lofty words and impressive wisdom to tell you God's secret plan.*
2 *For I decided that while I was with you I would forget everything except Jesus Christ, the one who was crucified.*
3 *I came to you in weakness – timid and trembling.*
4 *And my message and my preaching were very plain. Rather than using clever and*

persuasive speeches, I relied only on the
power of the Holy Spirit.
5 *I did this so you would trust not in human*
wisdom but in the power of God.
6 *Yet when I am among mature believers, I*
do speak with words of wisdom, but not the
kind of wisdom that belongs to this world
or to the rulers of this world, who are soon
forgotten.
7 *No, the wisdom we speak of is the mystery*
of God—his plan that was previously
hidden, even though he made it for our
ultimate glory before the world began.
8 *But the rulers of this world have not*
understood it; if they had, they would not
have crucified our glorious Lord.
9 *That is what the Scriptures mean when*
they say, "No eye has seen, no ear has
heard, and no mind has imagined what
God has prepared for those who love him."
10 *But it was to us that God revealed these*
things by his Spirit. For his Spirit searches
out everything and shows us God's deep
secrets.
11 *No one can know a person's thoughts*
except that person's own spirit, and no one
can know God's thoughts except God's
own Spirit.
12 *And we have received God's Spirit (not*
the world's spirit), so we can know the

wonderful things God has freely given us.
13 *When we tell you these things, we do not use words that come from human wisdom. Instead, we speak words given to us by the Spirit, using the Spirit's words to explain spiritual truths.*
14 *But people who aren't spiritual can't receive these truths from God's Spirit. It all sounds foolish to them and they can't understand it, for only those who are spiritual can understand what the Spirit means.*
15 *Those who are spiritual can evaluate all things, but they themselves cannot be evaluated by others.*
16 *For, "Who can know the LORD's thoughts? Who knows enough to teach him?" But we understand these things, for we have the mind of Christ.*
1 Corinthians 2:1-16 NLT

1 *Once you were dead because of your disobedience and your many sins.*
2 *You used to live in sin, just like the rest of the world, obeying the devil – the commander of the powers in the unseen world. He is the spirit at work in the hearts of those who refuse to obey God.*
3 *All of us used to live that way, following the passionate desires and inclinations of*

our sinful nature. By our very nature we were subject to God's anger, just like everyone else.
4 But God is so rich in mercy, and he loved us so much,
5 that even though we were dead because of our sins, he gave us life when he raised Christ from the dead. (It is only by God's grace that you have been saved!)
6 For he raised us from the dead along with Christ and seated us with him in the heavenly realms because we are united with Christ Jesus.
7 So God can point to us in all future ages as examples of the incredible wealth of his grace and kindness toward us, as shown in all he has done for us who are united with Christ Jesus.
8 God saved you by his grace when you believed. And you can't take credit for this; it is a gift from God.
9 Salvation is not a reward for the good things we have done, so none of us can boast about it.
10 For we are God's masterpiece. He has created us anew in Christ Jesus, so we can do the good things he planned for us long ago.
11 Don't forget that you Gentiles used to be outsiders. You were called "uncircumcised

heathens" by the Jews, who were proud of their circumcision, even though it affected only their bodies and not their hearts.
12 *In those days you were living apart from Christ. You were excluded from citizenship among the people of Israel, and you did not know the covenant promises God had made to them. You lived in this world without God and without hope.*
13 *But now you have been united with Christ Jesus. Once you were far away from God, but now you have been brought near to him through the blood of Christ.*
14 *For Christ himself has brought peace to us. He united Jews and Gentiles into one people when, in his own body on the cross, he broke down the wall of hostility that separated us.*
15 *He did this by ending the system of law with its commandments and regulations. He made peace between Jews and Gentiles by creating in himself one new people from the two groups.*
16 *Together as one body, Christ reconciled both groups to God by means of his death on the cross, and our hostility toward each other was put to death.*
17 *He brought this Good News of peace to you Gentiles who were far away from him, and peace to the Jews who were near.*

[18] *Now all of us can come to the Father through the same Holy Spirit because of what Christ has done for us.*
[19] *So now you Gentiles are no longer strangers and foreigners. You are citizens along with all of God's holy people. You are members of God's family.*
[20] *Together, we are his house, built on the foundation of the apostles and the prophets. And the cornerstone is Christ Jesus himself.*
[21] *We are carefully joined together in him, becoming a holy temple for the Lord.*
[22] *Through him you Gentiles are also being made part of this dwelling where God lives by his Spirit.*
Ephesians 2:1-22 NLT

[20] *I have been crucified with Christ; it is no longer I who live, but Christ lives in me; and the life which I now live in the flesh I live by faith in the Son of God, who loved me and gave Himself for me.*
Galatians 2:20 NKJV

11

THE CROSS OF JESUS AS A SPECTACLE FOR THE ALTAR OF SALVATION

In this chapter, we are going to see different categories of people who were signposted to Calvary Cross, while watching Jesus carrying His cross on His shoulder to Golgotha.

> [22] *And the key of the house of David will I lay upon his shoulder; so he shall open, and none shall shut; and he shall shut, and none shall open.*
> **Isaiah 22:22**

> [18] *I am He who lives, and was dead, and behold, I am alive forevermore. Amen. And I have the keys of Hades and of Death.*
> **Revelation 1:18**

The 27th chapter of the book Matthew gives us the details of different categories of people who saw Jesus carrying His cross, the supreme Altar of sacrifice for human redemption. I am highlighting this to demonstrate why we must amplify the message of the cross based on the statement that Jesus made in John 3:14-15 and John 12:32 that whosoever looks unto him on the cross and believes will have eternal life. It also underscores the fact that His being lifted on the cross will draw all categories of men to Himself. Indeed, one of the mysteries of the cross is that it has a supernatural drawing power. It is like a fishing rod to catch fish in the river.

> [14] *Just as Moses lifted up the [bronze] serpent in the desert [on a pole], so must the Son of Man be lifted up [on the cross],*
> [15] *so that whoever believes will in Him have eternal life [after physical death, and will actually live forever].*
> **John 3:14-15 AMP**

> [32] *And I, if I be lifted up from the earth, will draw all men unto me.*
> [33] *This he said, signifying what death he should die.*
> **John 12:32-33**

Thus, we shall examine Mathew 27 to draw out various people who were drawn and signposted to the Cross on the shoulder of Jesus, which symbolically fulfilled Isaiah 22:22. It reveals the categories of people that witnessed his journey to Calvary, with the Cross on His shoulder as 'SPECTACLE' pointing men to the Altar of God's redemptive sacrifice. The message of the cross today is still drawing many souls to Christ on daily basis. Hallelujah!

> 1 *When morning came, all the chief priests and the elders of the people took counsel against Jesus to put him to death.*
> 2 *And they bound him and led him away and delivered him over to Pilate the governor.*
> 3 *Then when Judas, his betrayer, saw that Jesus was condemned, he changed his mind and brought back the thirty pieces of silver to the chief priests and the elders,*
> 4 *saying, "I have sinned by betraying innocent blood." They said, "What is that to us? See to it yourself."*
> 5 *And throwing down the pieces of silver into the temple, he departed, and he went and hanged himself.*
> 6 *But the chief priests, taking the pieces of silver, said, "It is not lawful to put them into the treasury, since it is blood money."*
> 7 *So they took counsel and bought with*

them the potter's field as a burial place for
strangers.
8 *Therefore that field has been called the*
Field of Blood to this day.
9 *Then was fulfilled what had been spoken*
by the prophet Jeremiah, saying, "And
they took the thirty pieces of silver, the
price of him on whom a price had been set
by some of the sons of Israel,
10 *and they gave them for the potter's field,*
as the Lord directed me."
11 *Now Jesus stood before the governor, and*
the governor asked him, "Are you the King
of the Jews?" Jesus said, "You have said
so."
12 *But when he was accused by the chief*
priests and elders, he gave no answer.
13 *Then Pilate said to him, "Do you not hear*
how many things they testify against
you?"
14 *But he gave him no answer, not even to a*
single charge, so that the governor was
greatly amazed.
15 *Now at the feast the governor was*
accustomed to release for the crowd any
one prisoner whom they wanted.
16 *And they had then a notorious prisoner*
called Barabbas.
17 *So when they had gathered, Pilate said to*
them, "Whom do you want me to release

for you: Barabbas, or Jesus who is called Christ?"
[18] *For he knew that it was out of envy that they had delivered him up.*
[19] *Besides, while he was sitting on the judgment seat, his wife sent word to him, "Have nothing to do with that righteous man, for I have suffered much because of him today in a dream."*
[20] *Now the chief priests and the elders persuaded the crowd to ask for Barabbas and destroy Jesus.*
[21] *The governor again said to them, "Which of the two do you want me to release for you?" And they said, "Barabbas."*
[22] *Pilate said to them, "Then what shall I do with Jesus who is called Christ?" They all said, "Let him be crucified!"*
[23] *And he said, "Why? What evil has he done?" But they shouted all the more, "Let him be crucified!"*
[24] *So when Pilate saw that he was gaining nothing, but rather that a riot was beginning, he took water and washed his hands before the crowd, saying, "I am innocent of this man's blood; see to it yourselves."*
[25] *And all the people answered, "His blood be on us and on our children!"*
[26] *Then he released for them Barabbas, and*

having scourged Jesus, delivered him to be crucified.
27 *Then the soldiers of the governor took Jesus into the governor's headquarters, and they gathered the whole battalion before him.*
28 *And they stripped him and put a scarlet robe on him,*
29 *and twisting together a crown of thorns, they put it on his head and put a reed in his right hand. And kneeling before him, they mocked him, saying, "Hail, King of the Jews!"*
30 *And they spit on him and took the reed and struck him on the head.*
31 *And when they had mocked him, they stripped him of the robe and put his own clothes on him and led him away to crucify him.*
32 *As they went out, they found a man of Cyrene, Simon by name. They compelled this man to carry his cross.*
33 *And when they came to a place called Golgotha (which means Place of a Skull),*
34 *they offered him wine to drink, mixed with gall, but when he tasted it, he would not drink it.*
35 *And when they had crucified him, they divided his garments among them by casting lots.*

36 *Then they sat down and kept watch over*
him there.
37 *And over his head they put the charge*
against him, which read, "This is Jesus, the
King of the Jews."
38 *Then two robbers were crucified with*
him, one on the right and one on the left.
39 *And those who passed by derided him,*
wagging their heads
40 *and saying, "You who would destroy the*
temple and rebuild it in three days, save
yourself! If you are the Son of God, come
down from the cross."
41 *So also the chief priests, with the scribes*
and elders, mocked him, saying,
42 *"He saved others; he cannot save himself.*
He is the King of Israel; let him come down
now from the cross, and we will believe in
him.
43 *He trusts in God; let God deliver him*
now, if he desires him. For he said, 'I am the
Son of God.'"
44 *And the robbers who were crucified with*
him also reviled him in the same way.
45 *Now from the sixth hour there was*
darkness over all the land until the ninth
hour.
46 *And about the ninth hour Jesus cried out*
with a loud voice, saying, "Eli, Eli, lema
sabachthani?" that is, "My God, my God,

why have you forsaken me?"
47 *And some of the bystanders, hearing it, said, "This man is calling Elijah."*
48 *And one of them at once ran and took a sponge, filled it with sour wine, and put it on a reed and gave it to him to drink.*
49 *But the others said, "Wait, let us see whether Elijah will come to save him."*
50 *And Jesus cried out again with a loud voice and yielded up his spirit.*
51 *And behold, the curtain of the temple was torn in two, from top to bottom. And the earth shook, and the rocks were split.*
52 *The tombs also were opened. And many bodies of the saints who had fallen asleep were raised,*
53 *and coming out of the tombs after his resurrection they went into the holy city and appeared to many.*
54 *When the centurion and those who were with him, keeping watch over Jesus, saw the earthquake and what took place, they were filled with awe and said, "Truly this was the Son of God!"*
55 *There were also many women there, looking on from a distance, who had followed Jesus from Galilee, ministering to him,*
56 *among whom were Mary Magdalene and Mary the mother of James and Joseph and*

the mother of the sons of Zebedee.
57 *When it was evening, there came a rich man from Arimathea, named Joseph, who also was a disciple of Jesus.*
58 *He went to Pilate and asked for the body of Jesus. Then Pilate ordered it to be given to him.*
59 *And Joseph took the body and wrapped it in a clean linen shroud*
60 *and laid it in his own new tomb, which he had cut in the rock. And he rolled a great stone to the entrance of the tomb and went away.*
61 *Mary Magdalene and the other Mary were there, sitting opposite the tomb.* **Matthew 27:1-61 ESV**

From the above scripture, we can highlight the following people who saw Christ on His way to Calvary:

1. The chief priests (vs 1).
2. The lawmakers (Sanhedrin Council), scribes, and elders (vs 1).
3. The judge or governor, Pilate (vs 2).
4. On His way to Calvary cross, armed robbers and prisoners were there (vs 5,7,27-28).
5. The soldiers who spat on him, scourged him, beat him, put a platted crown of thorns on his head, and led him to be crucified (vs 16-20).
6. An African man whom they compelled to

carry Jesus' cross (vs 21).

7. Gamblers and betting gurus (vs 24).
8. Accusers were there on the way to the cross (vs 25-26).
9. Mockers and jesters were there (vs 29-32).
10. Medical professionals were there on His way to Calvary (vs 22-23,36).
11. A centurion who got born again on that very day (vs 39).
12. There were renown women who served the ministry of Jesus faithfully (vs 40-41,47; see also Luke 8:1-3).
13. A wealthy, rich businessman was there at Calvary who believed he was called to finance the burial of the body of Christ (vs 57-60).
14. A legal professional (Pharisee) called Nicodemus was also on the way to Calvary with Jesus (see John 19:38-42).

Notice that it was the religious leaders who handed Jesus over to the politicians to be judged. The religious leaders did not defend Him, instead they rejected and renounced Him. This is exactly what is happening today because Jesus is still being betrayed and renounced by some religious authorities. The Church of England, Episcopal Church in America, and even many Pentecostal, evangelical and charismatic churches are part of these groups who agreed with the politicians to endorse the agenda that the name of Jesus and the HOLY BIBLE should be taken out of our public life, in the guise of secularism. Many Bishops, even in the House of Lords, believe that God was wrong to recommend that marriage should only be between a man and a woman, endorsing same-sex unions, even though God's law stipulate that such is an abomination (Leviticus 18:21-25).

Evidently, God wants the message of the cross to be emphasised in these last days for the redemption of all. He allowed Jesus to carry His cross conspicuously as a spectacle before different categories of people, including the religious community. It is now our responsibility as the 21st century Church to preach and teach about the Calvary Cross as a spectacle pointing people to Jesus. When we preach about the cross as the altar of human redemption, Jesus will draw men and women to Himself.

Apostle Paul wrote in his Epistle to the Colossians that all the sins of humanity were cancelled on the cross, Satan and his demons were defeated on the cross, and redemptive victory was handed over to the Church (the Ecclesia).

> 13 *And you, being dead in your trespasses and the uncircumcision of your flesh, He has made alive together with Him, having forgiven you all trespasses,*
> 14 *having wiped out the handwriting of*

> *requirements that was against us, which was contrary to us. And He has taken it out of the way, having nailed it to the cross.*
> [15] *Having disarmed principalities and powers, He made a public spectacle of them, triumphing over them in it.*
> **Colossians 2:13-15 NKJV**

Glory to God for the sacrifice of Christ on the cross of calvary!

SONG:
All the way to Calvary
He went for me
Jesus went for me
He died to set me free

12

REDEMPTION OF HUMANITY FROM THE FOUR SPHERES OF SOCIAL STRATA TROUGH THE CROSS

In this chapter, we are going to look at four major areas where Satan can attack human destiny and how Jesus redeemed mankind through the finished work of the Cross, thereby securing our victory.

> 8 *Now when He had taken the scroll, the four living creatures and the twenty-four elders fell down before the Lamb, each having a harp, and golden bowls full of incense, which are the prayers of the saints.*
>
> 9 *And they sang a new song, saying:*
> *"You are worthy to take the scroll,*
> *And to open its seals;*
> *For You were slain,*
> *And have redeemed us to God by Your blood*

Out of every tribe and tongue and people and nation,
10 *And have made us kings and priests to our God;*
And we shall reign on the earth."
Revelation 5:8-10 NKJV

It is important to have good understanding of why the sacrifice of Jesus secured our redemption in these four areas of life. This will help believers to walk in the reality of their redemption irrespective of their tribe, language, people, or nation. The precious blood of Christ is effectual in these four dimensions because the destiny of every human being can be traced to these four major areas, generationally or genealogically. Because the sin of Adam corrupted every aspect of man's existence, it was imperative that the redemption Jesus, which He secured through the cross, had a lasting impact in these four spheres of human existence.

For us to appreciate the depth of what Jesus did on the cross, it is worthwhile we understand the definitions of these four dimensions of human existence: tribe, language, people and nation.

1. **TRIBE:** This refers to social divisions within a traditional society, consisting of families, or communities linked by social, economic, religious, or blood ties with a common culture and dialect, typically having a recognised leader.

2. **LANGUAGE:** This is the method of communication between people, either spoken or written, consisting of the use of words in a structured and conventional way. It is also defined as a system of communication used by a particular country or community, which can also be referenced as "mother tongue".
3. **PEOPLE:** This refers to human beings in general. It also means the members of a particular community or ethnic group. It represents a group of people that populate in or inhabit a place, for example a native of Canada, Amero Indian.
4. **NATION:** This is a large body of people united by common descent, history, culture, or language, inhabiting a particular country or territory, for instance England, Nigeria, Russia, Poland, India, France, Ireland, Scotland.

Again, the reason why Jesus had to channel His precious blood through these four areas is because the destiny of every human being can be traced to each of them. All the generations and dispensations of man have been corrupted by iniquity through Satan and his rebellious activities right from Adam until the arrival of second Adam, Jesus Christ. But through the sinless life of Christ and His holy blood, the iniquities of all generations of humanity have bene wiped off.

> [1] *The book of the ancestry (genealogy) of Jesus Christ (the Messiah, the Anointed), the son (descendant) of David, the son (descendant) of Abraham...*
> [17] *So all the generations from Abraham to David are fourteen, from David to the Babylonian exile (deportation) fourteen generations, from the Babylonian exile to the Christ fourteen generations.*
> **Matthew 1:1,17 AMPC**

In fact, the remaining genealogy from Adam to Abraham was recorded in Luke 3:22-38. No wonder John the Baptist referred to Jesus as the Lamb of God who takes away the sins of the world.

> [29] *The next day John saw Jesus coming toward him, and said, "Behold! The Lamb of God who takes away the sin of the world!*
> [36] *And looking at Jesus as He walked, he said, "Behold the Lamb of God!"*
> **John 1:29,36**

The same scripture was corroborated in the first epistle of Apostle Peter.

> [18] *You must know (recognize) that you were redeemed (ransomed) from the useless (fruitless) way of living inherited by tradition from [your] forefathers, not*

with corruptible things [such as] silver and gold,

[19] *But [you were purchased] with the precious blood of Christ (the Messiah), like that of a [sacrificial] lamb without blemish or spot.*

[20] *It is true that He was chosen and foreordained (destined and foreknown for it) before the foundation of the world, but He was brought out to public view (made manifest) in these last days (at the end of the times) for the sake of you.*

1 Peter 1:18-20 AMPC

All the four areas have been infiltrated by the activities of the kingdom of darkness from the fall of Adam, until Jesus shed his blood to deliver us.

[12] *Giving thanks unto the Father, which hath made us meet to be partakers of the inheritance of the saints in light:*

[13] *Who hath delivered us from the power of darkness, and hath translated us into the kingdom of his dear Son:*

[14] *In whom we have redemption through his blood, even the forgiveness of sins:*

Colossians 1:12-14

[9] *For in him dwelleth all the fulness of the Godhead bodily.*

10 And ye are complete in him, which is the head of all principality and power:...
13 And you, being dead in your sins and the uncircumcision of your flesh, hath he quickened together with him, having forgiven you all trespasses;
14 Blotting out the handwriting of ordinances that was against us, which was contrary to us, and took it out of the way, nailing it to his cross;
15 And having spoiled principalities and powers, he made a shew of them openly, triumphing over them in it.
Colossians 2:9-10,13-16

To triumph means to achieve a great victory or be successful. It is the depiction of a Roman general who conquers in battle and rides into ancient Rome after a victory. This is exactly what Jesus Christ accomplished on the cross for all tribes, languages, people, and nations. Hallelujah!

13

THE CROSS OF JESUS AS THE MOST IMPORTANT BRITISH CHRISTIAN HERITAGE

In the year 1992, I arrived in Great Britain to join my wife, Pastor Funmilola Akinfenwa. As my feet touched down at the Heathrow Airport, I heard the Spirit of the Lord say, "Son, you are welcome to your new place of assignment. I want you to give yourself to the study of British Church History and their Christian Heritage. This is because your Prophetic assignment will focus on rediscovering, re-digging, and the revival of the Ancient Christian Altars."

The Lord said that this would be the basis for bringing His glory back to the nation, and this will be achieved through the activities and influence of the Church in the nation. The Lord then gave me Genesis 26:17-22, Jeremiah 6:16, Isaiah 61:1-4 and Mathew 11:27-31 as the scriptural focus of my prophetic assignment in the land.

I logged this word in my spirit for almost a year because God did not tell me exactly what the statement meant. Being a Pastor from Nigeria, and a co-founder of a thriving church in Ibadan, Oyo state, I was thinking of establishing a branch of that Church in the UK in agreement with my senior pastor and mentor.

One day, as I prayed and sought direction on the plans to start the branch of the church, the Holy Spirit whispered to my ears exactly what He spoke to me in Heathrow the day I arrived in UK nearly two years earlier. He said, "Son, remember what I told you that this place, the UK, is a new place of assignment for you."

As I continued in prayer, I asked the same question Saul asked the Lord when he was slain on the road to Damascus: "Lord, what do you want to have me do?" (Acts 9:6). The Lord then replied clearly, "I am engaging you as Prophet and Prophetic Intercessor over the Nations, starting from the UK. You will raise armies of Prophetic Intercessors in this nation with the primary assignment to raise prayer altars for the restoration of Christian values and British Christian Heritage, which has been lost for several decades due to complacency, compromise, and spiritual lethargy in My churches in the land, especially Church of England. The enemy has taken advantage of this because the old generation of men and women who witnessed my major move in Revival failed to raise succeeding generations that would keep the fire burning. A generation has now emerged that never knew the God of their forefathers."

> [10] *After that generation died, another generation grew up who did not acknowledge the LORD or remember the mighty things he had done for Israel.*
> [11] *The Israelites did evil in the LORD's sight and served the images of Baal.*
> [12] *They abandoned the LORD, the God of their ancestors, who had brought them out of Egypt. They went after other gods, worshiping the gods of the people around them. And they angered the LORD.*
> [13] *They abandoned the LORD to serve Baal and the images of Ashtoreth.*
> [14] *This made the LORD burn with anger against Israel, so he handed them over to raiders who stole their possessions. He turned them over to their enemies all around, and they were no longer able to resist them.*
> **Judges 2:10-14 NLT**

The Lord then instructed me to devote my time to reading Church history and revivals in this nation and the Biography of their founding fathers. I read about the Wesley brothers and the Methodist Church, the Salvation Army formed by William and Caroline Booth, Charles Spurgeon, John Knox, St Patrick, John Buyon, the Jefferies Brothers, Evans, Smith Wigglesworth, and so on. The Lord said through these studies He will connect my heart to the hearts of the founding fathers of Great Britain. "Your heart must be married and knighted to this nation for you to be effective in your prophetic intercessory mission in this land," He said (Isaiah 62:4).

I also heard the Lord say one day, as I prayed, that "your assignment in this land will be like that of Isaac reopening the ancient wells of his heritage," as described in Genesis 26:15-25. "Through Prophetic intercession in My church, I will restore the Christian Heritage and prosperity of this nation. This will happen when the UK works in collaboration and in love with commonwealth citizens, especially Christians in the land."

In all my studies of Church history and British Christian Heritage, one thing has stood out to me: the symbolism of the "the CROSS and the National flag," which epitomises the faith, piety, and values of the national Patrons of each nation. What do I mean by this? All the national patrons of the Great Britain nations identified the symbolism of the CROSS and inculcated it into the national flags. These national patrons include St Georges (National

Patron of England), St Patrick (National Patron of Ireland), St David (National Patron of Wales), St Andrews (National Patron of Scotland) and St Piran (Patron father for Cornwall).

In the next chapter, I will briefly explore their biographies according to history and the symbol of their different flags and the nation they represent.

14

THE CROSS: UNITED KINGDOM'S NATIONAL PATRON'S FATHERS' SYMBOL OF FAITH IN CHRIST

In this chapter, we shall consider a panoramic survey of the Great Britain National Patrons and the CROSS in relation to the National Flag of the United Kingdom. The national flags of each of the four nations that constitute the United Kingdom conspicuously contain the symbol of CROSS. I believe all the national Patrons esteemed what Jesus accomplished on the cross for the atonement and redemption of humanity, and hence the cross became the foundational faith and belief in Christ. Although they lived at different centuries, the focal points of their faith were the same.

SAINT GEORGES... PATRON OF ENGLAND AND THE ENGLAND FLAG

Portrait by Hans von Kulmbach (circa 1510)

Saint George was regarded as the Martyred Patron of England. According to tradition, he was a soldier in the Roman army. He was a Cappadocian Greek origin and member of Praetorian Guard for Roman Emperor Diocletian. He was sentenced to death for refusing to recant his Christian faith (died 23rd April 303). He became one of the most venerated saints, especially venerated as a military saint since Crusades (Wikipedia).

The flag of England was derived from St George's Cross. The association of the red cross on white background as an emblem of England can be traced back to the Middle Ages, and it was used as a component in the design of the Union Flag in 1606. From 1606, it is used as the Union Flag of the England including Wales. From 1707 the Union Flag became the flag of kingdom of Great Britain.

HISTORICAL BACKGROUND OF THE UNION FLAG

Up until, 1603 both England and Scotland were governed by two separate monarchs with two separate flags. But when Queen Elizabeth I died (March 24th, 1603), there was a re-unification between England and Scotland under King James VI of Scotland. According to history, this was possible because Queen Elizabeth I was childless and before she died, she expressed a deathbed wish that her cousin, King James VI of Scotland, should be the heir to the throne.

But at this time, the English Flag was Red Cross on white background (St Georges Emblem). Saint Georges happened to be the Patron Saint of England. The Scottish flag then was white diagonal cross on a blue background. It was derived from St Andrews cross (Scotland Patron saints). But as a sign of unification between England and Scotland, King James created a new banner by fully superimposing the English flag upon the Scottish flag. This became known as The Union Flag. This combination became symbolic banner up till 1707. Then during the reign of Queen Anne, the parliament of England and

Scotland were untied to form the new nation of Great Britain, and Queen Anne officially adopted the 101 years old banner as the national flag of newly created nation (GB).

English National Flag

White background with red horizontal and vertical lines

TEN FASCINATING FACTS ABOUT SAINT ANDREW, THE NATIONAL PATRON OF SCOTLAND

1. Andrew was a Galilean fisherman before he and his brother Simon Peter became disciples of Jesus Christ.
2. He was crucified by the Romans on an X-shaped cross at Patras in Greece and, hundreds of years later, his remains were moved to Constantinople and then, in the 13th century, to Amalfi in southern Italy where they are kept to this day.

3. Legend has it that a Greek monk, known as St Rule or St Regulus, was ordered in a vision to take a few relics of Andrew to the 'ends of the earth' for safe keeping. He set off on a sea journey to eventually come ashore on the coast of Fife at a settlement which is now the modern town of St Andrews.

4. In 832 AD Andrew is said to have appeared in a vision to a Pictish king the night before a battle against the Northumbrians in what is now the village of Athelstaneford in East Lothian. On the day of the battle a Saltire, an X-shaped cross, appeared in the sky above the battlefield and the Picts were victorious.

5. The Saltire, or Saint Andrew's Cross, was subsequently adopted as the national emblem and flag of the Scots.

6. Andrew was first recognised as an official patron saint of Scotland in 1320 at the signing of the Declaration of Arbroath an appeal to the Pope by Scottish noblemen asserting Scotland's independence from England.

7. The presence of Andrew's relics in Scotland - a tooth, a kneecap, arm, and finger bones - meant that St Andrews became a popular medieval pilgrimage site although they were destroyed in the 16th century during the Scottish Reformation.

8. In 1879 the Archbishop of Amalfi gifted Andrew's shoulder blade to St Mary's Cathedral in Edinburgh. Pope Paul VI donated further relics in 1969.

9. Andrew is also the patron saint of Greece, Russia, Romania, and Barbados. Remnants of the cross he was crucified on remain in the St Andrew's Cathedral Patras in Greece. Saint Andrew was the first bishop there and then crucified by the Romans.

10. His patronage extends to fishmongers, gout, singers, sore throats, spinsters, maidens, old maids and women wishing to become mothers.

Scottish National Flag Of St Andrews

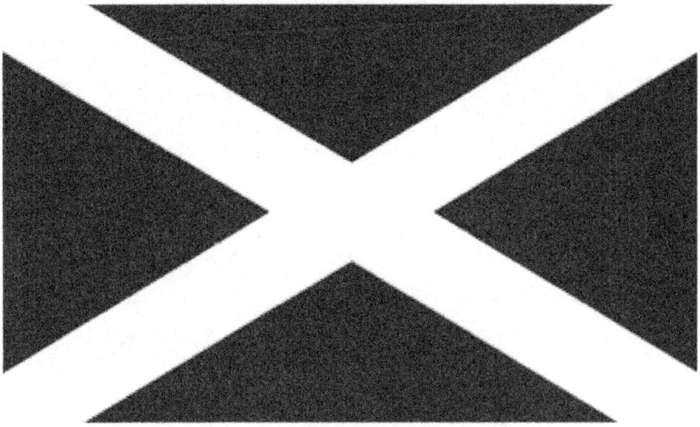

Blue background with diagonal white cross

In 1801, when Ireland became a part of Great Britain, the Union Flag was re-designed to include the cross of St Patrick (Patron saint of Ireland) which was a red diagonal cross on white background.

Irish National Flag (St Patrick)

White background with red diagonal crosses

The combination of all the three flags formed the national flag of the United Kingdom - English, Scottish, Irish, and Welsh. This is what is known as The Union Jack Flag.

If the flag of the nation, symbolised by the CROSS, reflects the nation's strength, beliefs, values, and identity, then the churches in the UK need to go back to the message of the cross. Our founding fathers built their faith, hope and righteousness upon what JESUS did on the cross of Calvary. That was the reason why they chose to lift up the cross of Jesus Christ as a symbol for our national identity. Not only that, but it also showed that all the Patron Saints were united in common faith based upon the finished work of Christ on Calvary Cross.

Flag of Saint David

Traditionally, in both protestant and Catholic tradition, crossed emblems have only been allocated to those martyred in the name of Christianity.

The flag of Saint David (the patron saint of Wales), a yellow cross on a black field, is used in the emblem of St David's. In recent times, the flag has been adopted as a symbol of Welsh nationalism. Some organisations, such as the Christian party, use this flag instead of the dragon Draig Goch. In fact, it was used as the emblem of Welsh National football jersey and was worn during the European Championship 2016.

The flag of St. David did not become part of public consciousness of the Welsh until 1994 and is used primarily to display dissatisfaction with the current flag. It has since become a famous symbol of Welsh patriotism alongside the Red Dragon, rather than in direct competition with it.

The flag of the church in Wales is Blue Cross on white field.

The Flag of St David

SAINT PIRAN: PATRON OF CORNWALL

Saint Piran was a 5th century Cornish Abbot and Saint. He died in 480 AD. He was supposedly of Irish Origin. He was the Patron Saint of tin tin-miners, and generally regarded as the Patron saint of Cornwall, although Saint Michael and Saint Petroc also have some claim to this title.

Saint Phiran was the most famous of all the saints said to have come to Cornwall from Ireland on the 5th century. March 5th is the traditional feast day of both St Phiran and because the Irish saint of Ciaran of Saigir, who founded the monastery at Seir-Kieran in County Offlay. For this reason, March 5th of every year is set apart in both Cornwall and Ireland, hence feast day for both St Ciaran of Saigar and Saint Piran. In perranzabuloe parish, Piran Feast is traditionally celebrated on the last Monday in October.

LEGENDS

The heathen Irish tied him to a mill-stone, rolled it over the edge of a cliff into a stormy sea. The sea immediately became calm, and the saint (St Phiran) floated safely over the water to land upon the sandy beach of Perranzabuloe (Peranporth) in Cornwall. His first disciples were said to have been a badger, a fix and a bear. He landed in Cornwall, and there established himself as a hermit. His sanctity and his austerity won for him the veneration of all around, and the gift of miracles, with which he was favoured, brought many to seek his charitable aid. He was joined at Perranzabuloe by his Christian converts and together they founded the Abbey of Lanpiran, with Phiran as Abbot. St Piran re-discovered tin-smelting (tin had been smelted in Cornwall since before the Roman arrival, but the methods had since been lost), when his black hearthstone, which was evidently a slab of tin-bearing ore, had the tin smelt out of it and rise to the top in the form of a white cross (thus the image on the flag, a white cross on black field). This happened to be a miracle DEATH AND VENERATION OF ST PHIRAN. He died was buried in Perranzabuloe in 480AD his remains were subsequently exhumed and re-distributed to be venerated in various reliquaries. Exeter Cathedral was reputed to be the possessor of one of his arms. According to an inventory, St Piran Old Church, Perranzabuloe had

had reliquary containing his head and also the hearse in which his body was placed in processional.

THE FLAG OF SAINT PIRAN

The earliest documented design of St Piran's flag is known to be white cross in a black field. This represents Cornish identity, a white smouldering (tin-smelt) cross coming out of black tin- bearing ore. St Phiran erected a black hearthstone slab of tin-bearing ore, suddenly smelt out a shining (glittering) white tin cross. This happened in the outside where there was intense heat of the sun.

Cornish

15

EMPEROR CONSTANTINE THE GREAT AND HIS VISION OF THE CROSS

Constantinus, the emperor of Western Europe, which comprised of Spain, Gaul, and Britain, was the father of Constantine. He died on the 25th of July 306 in York, England. His death left a vacuum on the throne regarding who would succeed him. But by the collective agreement of his father's army, Constantine was appointed the new emperor to take over his late father's role.

However, Constantine was confronted with a big challenge of legitimising this role in Rome, with the people and the authority - the Emperor of Eastern Europe, Augustus, and Ceacers. According to history, his father had told him several times that though they worship many idols in Rome, there is a Supreme Being somewhere above the sky who is greater than any known god.

One night, Constantine called on this unknown God with earnest prayer to reveal to him who he was and stretch forth his right hand to help him in his present difficulties. While he was thus praying with fervent entreaty, a most extraordinary sign appeared to him from heaven about noon, when the day was already beginning to decline; he saw with his own eyes the sign of a cross of light in the heavens, above the sun, and bearing the inscription, "By this symbol you will conquer." Constantine was struck with amazement by the sight, and his whole army witnessed the miracle.

Constantine was unsure what this appearance of the cross on the sky could mean, but he continued to ponder all day long until the night when he slept. In his sleep, the Christ of God appeared to him with the same sign which he had seen in the heavens previously in the noon day.

According to the story, Jesus commanded him to make a likeness of that sign which he had seen in the heavens, and to use it as a safeguard in all engagements with his enemies.

When he rose from his sleep, he told his friends about the encounter. Then he called together the workers in gold and precious stones, sat amongst them, and described to them the sign he had seen, telling them to represent it in gold and precious stones. They should also engrave it on his own shield and the shield of all his army. Afterwards, he led his armies against his opposition and won the battle, thereby fulfilling what Jesus told him in the vision encounter, "by this cross you shall win."

The emperor constantly made use of this sign of salvation as a safeguard against every adverse and hostile power. He was the first Roman emperor to profess Christianity. Not only did he initiate the evolution of the empire into a Christian state, he also provided the impulse for a distinctively Christian culture that prepared the way for the growth of Byzantine and Western medieval culture.

Later in life, Constantine had the habit of delivering edifying sermons, which he would compose in Latin and pronounce in Greek. From 303, during the great persecution of the Christians that began at the court of Diocletian at Nicomedia and was enforced with particular intensity in the eastern parts of the empire, Christianity was a major issue of public policy.

Throughout his life, Constantine ascribed his success to his conversion to Christianity and the support of the Christian God. The triumphal arch erected in his honour at Rome after the defeat of Maxentius ascribed the victory to the "inspiration of the Divinity" as well as to Constantine's own genius. A statue set up at the same time showed Constantine himself holding aloft a cross and the legend, "By this saving sign I have delivered your city from the tyrant and restored liberty to the Senate and people of Rome."

If Jesus could appear to an unbelieving idol worshipping Emperor, telling him in a vision to put his faith on the power of the "CROSS," then we, the Ecclesia, should do the same with full understanding of its significance.

As the Body of Christ globally, there are a lot of battles and challenges we are confronted with in this wicked world. However, victory is guaranteed as we look up unto Jesus and His finished work on the cross of Calvary. By His Cross we shall win!

> [18] *For the message of the cross is foolishness to those who are perishing, but to us who are being saved it is the power of God.*
> **1 Corinthians 1:18**

Hallelujah!

16

APPLYING THE POWER OF THE CROSS IN PRAYER

In this chapter, we will explore how to use the application of the power of the cross in prayer. We would also examine how Prophet Elisha demonstrated the power that foreshadowed the application of the power of the cross to recover a lost axe from the sea of Jordan.

Restoring The Lost Axe Head

> 1 *And the sons of the prophets said to Elisha, "See now, the place where we dwell with you is too small for us.*
> 2 *Please, let us go to the Jordan, and let every man take a beam from there, and let us make there a place where we may dwell." So he answered, "Go."*

> [3] *Then one said, "Please consent to go with your servants." And he answered, "I will go."*
> [4] *So he went with them. And when they came to the Jordan, they cut down trees.*
> [5] *But as one was cutting down a tree, the iron ax head fell into the water; and he cried out and said, "Alas, master! For it was borrowed."*
> [6] *So the man of God said, "Where did it fall?" And he showed him the place. So he cut off a stick, and threw it in there; and he made the iron float.*
> [7] *Therefore he said, "Pick it up for yourself." So he reached out his hand and took it.*
> **2 Kings 6:1-7 NKJV**

In the passage, we see how Prophet Elisha demonstrated the power of the cross when he retrieved the lost axe head from the river Jordan. Satan tried to stagnate or stop the building project embarked upon by the sons of Prophet, but the power of the cross recovered the axe head to the glory of God.

Figuratively, the axe head represents man as God's battle axe in our day. Man lost his position before God through the sin of Adam and Eve. But through the finished work of Christ on the cross,

God has redeemed man from the captivity and kingdom of Satan.

> 22 *Then the LORD God said, "Behold, the man has become like one of Us, to know good and evil. And now, lest he put out his hand and take also of the tree of life, and eat, and live forever" –*
> 23 *therefore the LORD God sent him out of the garden of Eden to till the ground from which he was taken.*
> 24 *So He drove out the man; and He placed cherubim at the east of the garden of Eden, and a flaming sword which turned every way, to guard the way to the tree of life.*
> **Genesis 3:22-24 NKJV**

As we have already seen from the above text, mankind was driven from the presence of God into the world governed by Satan and his demons. Humanity was lost in the deep sea of iniquity and hence Satan's captivity and slavery. Man was lost into Satan's kingdom of darkness for almost 4,000 years without any hope of salvation. The purpose of God for man as the ruler and the king of the earth with kingdom authority was sabotaged.

However, the omnipotent God who knows the end from the beginning put into place an eternal plan to rescue man like the lost "axe head" that fell into the sea. God prepared an eternal stick (the cross of Calvary) to pull man out of the sea of sin and eternal damnation. This is exactly what prophet Elisha demonstrated when he threw the stick into the river and made the lost axe head float, restoring it to its rightful owner.

> [5] *As one of them was cutting down a tree, the iron axhead fell into the water. "Oh no, my lord!" he cried out. "It was borrowed!"*
> [6] *The man of God asked, "Where did it fall?" When he showed him the place, Elisha cut a stick and threw it there, and made the iron float.*
> **2 King 6:5-6**

The scenario here looks ridiculous and foolish to human understanding. In fact, according to the simple Archimedes law of floatation, the stick was supposed to float on the water. But supernaturally, the stick went down to the bottom of the river, located the axe head, brought out the axe head, and restored the axe head so it could continue to perform the purpose for which it was made. The supernatural power to restore the lost axe head rested in the stick which is symbolic of the Calvary cross. It was able to restore the axe so it could continue the expansion of God's work.

Jesus Himself prophesied about the tree of the cross upon which He will be lifted up to draw out men (God's Battles axes) from the ocean of sins to become the instrument by which God will establish His Kingdom on the earth.

> [31] *Now is the judgment of this world; now the ruler of this world will be cast out.*
> [32] *And I, if I am lifted up from the earth, will draw all peoples to Myself."*
> [33] *This He said, signifying by what death He would die.*
> **John 12:31-33 NKJV**

Over 2000 years ago, the cross of calvary became the demonstration of the power of God for the salvation of humanity. It looked foolish to Satan, but it turned out to be the wisdom and the power of God that inflicted maximum defeat and destruction on the devil's kingdom.

> [17] *For Christ did not send me to baptize, but to preach the gospel – not with wisdom and eloquence, lest the cross of Christ be emptied of its power.*
> [18] *For the message of the cross is foolishness to those who are perishing, but to us who are being saved it is the power of God.*
> **1 Corinthians 1:17-18**

The cross of Calvary was designed by God to facilitate the restoration of man as God's image and battle axe. Prophet Elisha saw the picture of "Calvary stick" as a means to restore the lost axe head from the river. The power of the cross turned around the hopeless situation to the praise and glory of God, thereby putting the devil to shame. Hallelujah!

> [12] *giving thanks to the Father who has qualified us to be partakers of the inheritance of the saints in the light.*
> [13] *He has delivered us from the power of darkness and conveyed us into the kingdom of the Son of His love,*
> [14] *in whom we have redemption through His blood, the forgiveness of sins…*
> [19] *For it pleased the Father that in Him all the fullness should dwell,*
> [20] *and by Him to reconcile all things to Himself, by Him, whether things on earth or things in heaven, having made peace through the blood of His cross.*
> [21] *And you, who once were alienated and enemies in your mind by wicked works, yet now He has reconciled*
> [22] *in the body of His flesh through death, to present you holy, and blameless, and above reproach in His sight.*
>
> **Colossians 1:12-14,19-22 NKJV**

Let the church of Jesus arise! We have been created and fashioned in Christ as God's battle axes to carry out good work and to advance the kingdom of God the earth.

> [10] *For we are His workmanship, created in Christ Jesus for good works, which God prepared beforehand that we should walk in them.*
> **Ephesians 2:10 NKJV**

We are God's battles axes and the Cyrus of our day.

> [20] *"You are My battle-ax and weapons of war: For with you I will break the nation in pieces; With you I will destroy kingdoms;*
> [21] *With you I will break in pieces the horse and its rider; With you I will break in pieces the chariot and its rider;*
> [22] *With you also I will break in pieces man and woman; With you I will break in pieces old and young; With you I will break in pieces the young man and the maiden;*
> [23] *With you also I will break in pieces the shepherd and his flock; With you I will break in pieces the farmer and his yoke of oxen; And with you I will break in pieces governors and rulers.*

> [24] *"And I will repay Babylon And all the inhabitants of Chaldea For all the evil they have done in Zion in your sight," says the LORD.*
> [25] *"Behold, I am against you, O destroying mountain, Who destroys all the earth," says the LORD. "And I will stretch out My hand against you, Roll you down from the rocks, And make you a burnt mountain.*
> **Jeremiah 51:20-25 NKJV**

Let us earnestly pray that God would once again pour out the Cyrus anointing upon the Ecclesia!

> [1] *"Thus says the LORD to His anointed, To Cyrus, whose right hand I have held – To subdue nations before him And loose the armor of kings, To open before him the double doors, So that the gates will not be shut:*
> [2] *'I will go before you And make the crooked places straight; I will break in pieces the gates of bronze And cut the bars of iron.*
> [3] *I will give you the treasures of darkness And hidden riches of secret places, That you may know that I, the LORD, Who call you by your name, Am the God of Israel.*
> [4] *For Jacob My servant's sake, And Israel*

My elect, I have even called you by your
name; I have named you, though you have
not known Me.
5 *I am the LORD, and there is no other;*
There is no God besides Me. I will gird you,
though you have not known Me,
6 *That they may know from the rising of the*
sun to its setting That there is none besides
Me. I am the LORD, and there is no other.
Isaiah 45:1-6 NKJV

1 *The Spirit of the Sovereign LORD is*
upon me, for the LORD has anointed me
to bring good news to the poor. He has sent
me to comfort the brokenhearted and to
proclaim that captives will be released and
prisoners will be freed.
2 *He has sent me to tell those who mourn*
that the time of the LORD's favor has
come, and with it, the day of God's anger
against their enemies.
3 *To all who mourn in Israel, he will give a*
crown of beauty for ashes, a joyous
blessing instead of mourning, festive
praise instead of despair. In their
righteousness, they will be like great oaks
that the LORD has planted for his own
glory.
4 *They will rebuild the ancient ruins,*

repairing cities destroyed long ago. They will revive them, though they have been deserted for many.
Isaiah 61:1-4 NLT

God also used Moses to demonstrate how the power of the cross has the capacity to turn bitter water to sweet.

[22] *So Moses brought Israel from the Red sea, and they went out into the wilderness of Shur; and they went three days in the wilderness, and found no water.*
[23] *And when they came to Marah, they could not drink of the waters of Marah, for they were bitter: therefore the name of it was called Marah.*
[24] *And the people murmured against Moses, saying, What shall we drink?*
[25] *And he cried unto the LORD; and the LORD shewed him a tree, which when he had cast into the waters, the waters were made sweet: there he made for them a statute and an ordinance, and there he proved them.*
Exodus 15:22-25

The tree that God showed Moses symbolises the cross of Christ. When the Cross is applied to any bitter situation, the power of God turns it around into joy and sweetness.

PRAYER: In the name of Jesus and by the power of the cross soaked with the blood of Jesus, I pray that every situation in my life that never produce sweet fruit be reversed in Jesus' name.
I pray that God of divine intervention will step into my case for a supernatural turn around. Amen!

INTRODUCING THE ORDER OF THE CROSS OF JESUS

Description: A group of men and women who affirm that the death of Jesus on the cross, His burial, and resurrection on the third day have achieved salvation for humanity and that Christ invites everyone to believe in Him and be saved.

- We believe that as Christians we share in Christ's invitation by being witnesses to Him in our sphere of influence based on the finished work on the cross.
- The cross of Christ is used in the letters of St Paul to refer to Christ's death, burial, and resurrection. The cross also signifies the daily dying to self that Christ asks of us.
- The Church has used the symbolism of the cross for the past 2000 years to reiterate these messages and to proclaim Christ's pre-eminence and Lordship.

- Christians have worn the cross since time immemorial to identify themselves as believers in and followers of Jesus Christ.

OUR AIM IN TODAY'S WORLD

To be living witnesses to the message of the cross, proclaiming it in our churches and communities, and living it out daily in our sphere of life.

OUR RULE OF LIFE

Aspiring every day to live a cross-shaped life, a life that proclaims the death, burial, and resurrection of Christ in our words and deeds. Indeed, Christianity is all about the finished work of Christ on Calvary.

As a physical sign of this, we shall wear the cross of Christ everyday as faithful witnesses to His death, burial, and resurrection, and as a sign of our own mortality and reminder that we die daily to this sinful world.

> [1] *And you hath he quickened, who were dead in trespasses and sins;*
> [2] *Wherein in time past ye walked according to the course of this world, according to the prince of the power of the air, the spirit that now worketh in the children of disobedience:*
> [3] *Among whom also we all had our conversation in times past in the lusts of our flesh, fulfilling the desires of the flesh*

and of the mind; and were by nature the children of wrath, even as others.

4 But God, who is rich in mercy, for his great love wherewith he loved us,

5 Even when we were dead in sins, hath quickened us together with Christ, (by grace ye are saved;)

6 And hath raised us up together, and made us sit together in heavenly places in Christ Jesus:

7 That in the ages to come he might shew the exceeding riches of his grace in his kindness toward us through Christ Jesus.

8 For by grace are ye saved through faith; and that not of yourselves: it is the gift of God:

9 Not of works, lest any man should boast.

10 For we are his workmanship, created in Christ Jesus unto good works, which God hath before ordained that we should walk in them.

11 Wherefore remember, that ye being in time past Gentiles in the flesh, who are called Uncircumcision by that which is called the Circumcision in the flesh made by hands;

12 That at that time ye were without Christ, being aliens from the commonwealth of Israel, and strangers from the covenants of promise, having no hope, and without God in the world:

13 *But now in Christ Jesus ye who sometimes were far off are made nigh by the blood of Christ.*

14 *For he is our peace, who hath made both one, and hath broken down the middle wall of partition between us.*

(Ephesians 2:1-14)

For further information,
Email: johnson44akinfenwa@gmail.com
Website: www.vopio.org

Printed in Great Britain
by Amazon

51915168R00109